One Of the Greatest Generation

One Of the Greatest Generation

Ronald Soucy

iUniverse, Inc.
New York Lincoln Shanghai

One Of the Greatest Generation

iUniverse, Inc.

For information address:
iUniverse, Inc.
2021 Pine Lake Road, Suite 100
Lincoln, NE 68512
www.iuniverse.com

ISBN: 0-595-28206-7 (pbk)
ISBN: 0-595-65745-1 (cloth)

Printed in the United States of America

"This book, I hope, will in some small way Pay tribute to those men and women who have given us the lives we have today—an American family portrait album of The greatest generation."

—Tom Brokaw
From the flyleaf of his
book, *"The Greatest Generation"*

Contents

IT is common knowledge that the language used by service men during WW II was liberally sprinkled with profanity. This is not to say that all used profanity, but many did. I was one of the worst. Having said that, I've chosen to refrain from that practice in writing of my time in the Navy. Profanity is only used where it is necessary. Also, the names of people and places are accurate unless the use of someone's real name could cause embarrassment for them, or a relative, today.

1

The Early Years

1925 was a good year in many ways. Calvin Coolidge was President, Red Grange was burning up football yardage for Illinois, Babe Ruth was hitting homeruns, and I was born. Collinsville, Connecticut was the village, and a Company house on Church Street was the place. Joan was six years old, and Denis, Jr. would be four in three weeks. My mother, Florence, was a World War I war bride from England. My father, Denis, now working in the Collins Company, had been a Canadian soldier.

How can I give you a feel for Collinsville? The Farmington River runs through it. The Collins Company is built along the riverbank on the Eastside, and the village houses dot the hills on both sides of the river. Many of those houses are two family duplexes, built and owned by the Company.

As you would readily guess, there is a bridge spanning the river, connecting both sides of the town. I was born on Church Street on the West side of the bridge, which is about five minutes walk to the center of town on the other side of the river. On our side of town there were two mom and pop grocery stores. On Main Street there were four stores selling groceries. Three were family owned, the other a chain store, the "First National". Also on Main Street there were three Barber shops, a clothing store, a toy store, a hardware store, two drug stores and a bank. The Post Office was located on a side street along with a combined tavern and candy store, another chain grocery store, the "A & P", and a butcher shop. Across the street from the First National Store, there was a furniture store owned by the local mortician. Three school buildings were a block off Main Street, adjacent to the Congregational Church Building. They were two story buildings constructed of wood. One had rooms for the first four grades, grades one and two downstairs, and upstairs, third and fourth grades. The janitor's room and lavatories were in the basement. Fifty feet away was a similar building with fifth and sixth grades downstairs, seventh and eighth upstairs. On the other side of the schoolyard, high school classes were taught in an old building, also constructed of wood.

If you were wondering where Church Street got its name, the Catholic Church was at the bottom of the street on the right corner. If I remember correctly, there were three of the Company owned duplex homes on each side of the street. We lived in the duplex at the top on the right. There were four rooms downstairs; kitchen, with a pantry, (the bathroom off the kitchen), dining room, parlor, and my parent's bedroom with my crib in there. Joan and Junior had the two bedrooms upstairs. I don't recall how old I was when I began to share the bedroom with Junior, but I have several memories related to being in that crib, and quite a few memories related to living on Church Street. (We moved across the river when I was five).

That was a good period in my life. My mother loved babies, and I was the baby for four years. I think my father loved me then, too. There is a memory of him taking me onto his lap and singing, "Sonny Boy" to me. Like the boy in the song, I must have been three years old. It may be that a Freudian Psychiatrist would see something significant in the memories I have of those first years. For me they are there, unconnected events from that period before we moved across the river. Since sexuality is so much a part of us, however, two of the memories are worth telling. One has to do with the water pistols Junior and I had when I was about three. They were the kind with a rubber bulb on the end, which you squeezed, and then released, while the barrel was in a glass of water. With the bulb filled, when you squeezed, it shot a thin stream of water quite a distance. Junior and I were playing outside one evening. I got the idea of sticking the loaded pistol out through my fly and shooting a stream. Junior thought that was hilarious. I felt proud, until my mother saw me out the window, and in anger made me get in the house, telling me I was a dirty pig. Another time during that period I had a sensitive place on the end of my penis. The foreskin was inflamed, and my mother

Saw me fidgeting. She asked me what was the matter, and I replied, "You'll be mad if I tell you." She responded, "No, I won't." So I showed her, and to my glad surprise, she wasn't angry. Where do you suppose a three year old gets the idea that anything related to his penis will make his mother angry? In ways like that mother's wrongly teach their children about their sexuality.

A couple of months after my fourth birthday, my mother sent me down to the Magnusson's apartment over Reichert's store. That wasn't a usual kind of thing, but at that stage I never questioned what my mother told me to do. That came later. The Magnusson's had lived in the duplex next to ours, but had moved to the apartment over Reichert's store. The store was at the bottom of the hill and one block to the left, facing the bridge that crossed the river. Mr. & Mrs. Magnusson were a delightful Swedish couple with three daughters. Margaret was married, and worked at the Post Office. Elsie had drowned in the river sometime before my memory begins. Mildred was a high school student. When I got to their apartment that day, Margaret was there, and when I arrived she kissed me exuberantly, and in the process accidentally stuck her finger in my eye. Later in the day when they sent me home, there was a new baby waiting. November 20, 1929 my sister Patricia was born. I have no memories, either positive or negative related to the event, unless it was Margaret's finger in my eye. Nothing had ever been mentioned about a new baby coming on the scene. So her arrival was a complete surprise to me. Not all at once, but after a while it was clear that I was no longer the center of mom's attention.

When I was five years old, we moved across the river to a house on High Street, the last street at the top of town on the East side of the river. This was also a duplex, but not Company owned. The house was at the South end of High Street, facing South Street, which went down past the Congregational Church and the school, three minutes walk from where we now lived. I have no idea of why we made that move. I wonder why I never thought to ask? Very early, I think, there was the lesson that some things weren't any of my business. I guess new babies, and the reasons for moving were both in that category. I have no idea what the rent cost in the Company house. I do know that it was $15 a month in the new place

The Depression had begun, but I don't recall anyone using that word to describe things. My father worked in the Grind Shop at the Collins Company grinding axes. During the early part of the Depression he was working two and a half days a week. Years later, I recall my mother once saying that there was a period then when his pay was $8.50 a week. Not owing money, and paying bills on time, was very important to my mother. In looking back, I wonder how they made it? Paying $15 monthly for rent when one's income is $8.50 a week has to be difficult. But that worry was never passed on to the children. We knew that times were hard, and there wasn't money for things like new clothes, but we never missed a meal. In all honesty, I need to add that I would have chosen to miss some of those meals if I had a choice. Had I complained, however, I would have gotten a "back hander". My mother was a good cook, and she did the best she could with what she had. However, her "Spanish Rice" made me gag. I would have settled for a slice of bread on the occasions when that was the meal. But that choice was not open to me, and I gagged down many meals of "Spanish Rice".

School began for me right after my sixth birthday. There was no Kindergarten, and first grade was my introduction. I liked it! Miss Peterson was the teacher who taught me to read. I have fond memories of her. When the school year was over, and we were promoted to the second grade, it came as good news that Miss Peterson would be teaching that class. The grading system consisted of; Excellent, Good, Fair, Poor, or U (for unsatisfactory). From Miss Peterson I received excellent grades.

Something happened to me by the time school began for my third year. Still in my memory is one morning that autumn when it was time to leave for school. My little sister, Pat, was standing on the bank waving goodbye as I started down

South Street, and I felt like crying. I did not want to go to school. That was something new. I had not had that feeling during those first two years. School was out each day at 3:45. There were occasions that year when seated at my desk I'd look out the window longing for the day to be over. Nobody knew how I felt. It wasn't something I could talk about at home. It was one of those things in life for which there is no solution, the kind of thing that can only be endured. Out of that experience grew the feeling that in many ways I was on my own.

There were no expressions of affection in the family when one was no longer the "baby". There were no hugs, or anything communicated which would mean, "I love you just because you are you". We received approval when we did things, like receiving good report cards, and great disapproval for many other things. I never saw my mother and father embrace each other. If my father was leaving the house he would give my mother a quick kiss, but there were no words of affection exchanged. There were arguments, however. It was an open stairway up to the room Junior and I shared, and sometimes we would be wakened at night to the sound of mom and dad in a bitter argument. Mom was a small woman, five feet two inches, and weighing 98 pounds. I was afraid that in anger he would physically abuse her. He never did as far as I know. But the arguments were bitter, and increasingly so as the years went by.

My father's main interest was the sport of boxing. One of the family stories was of him having a boxing match with a fighter named "Tom Mix" shortly after arriving in Canada after WW I.

He was soundly defeated, but in a return match he won. Beginning before I was born dad was the trainer-manager of several fighters. During the summer months, prizefights were held weekly, weather permitting, in Hartford, and Torrington. Quite often, one or more of the fellows my father was managing would be on one of those cards. Nelson Chartier was one of the young fighters, and he was outstanding. He won the featherweight championship at the Golden Gloves in the early 1930's. Then, instead of turning professional he stopped fighting.

It was understood in the family that Junior was going to be a prizefighter. There was never any question of that. What Junior thought about it did not matter. I doubt that anyone ever asked him. Not very long after adolescence he began training.

On the other hand, I was a skinny child, and it was very clear that I wasn't going to be a fighter. I detested schoolyard fights, and avoided them if at all possible. In the give and take of growing up, getting into a fight with someone at school was inevitable, but I usually lost such encounters. Then at home I would lie about the source of the black eye if I happened to get one. I was avoiding dad's disapproval. It was a difficult place for me to be. I was afraid of fighting, and disliked myself for being afraid. Good grades came easily for me in most subjects, but back then I would have exchanged my brain for sawdust if I could have been a prizefighter, and thus, in my mind, win the approval of my father, approval that just wasn't there for me. There is a memory that illustrates well how it was. During the summer months the fighters sparred at an outdoor ring that was built at a clearing in the woods above our house. Often, men from town would come to watch the fighters train. One summer evening among those watching were some visitors from Hartford who were connected to prize fighting: Pete Perrone, who was promoter of the fights in Hartford, and Lenny Maurillo who was manager of Willie Pep during the early years of his spectacular career. Most of the time I avoided going up there for fear that my father would have me put on the gloves, and fight with some boy who was present. On this particular evening, with the visitors from Hartford there, I felt it was safe so I eased my way, unobtrusively I hoped, into the group of watchers gathered around the ring. As I did, my father, indicating me with his head, said, "We're going to make a poet out of this one." All the men chuckled. If my father had slapped me it wouldn't have been more painful.

During those growing years, the Trinity Episcopal Church was a big part of the weekly schedule for Joan, Junior, and me. Both Sunday School, and worship services following, were something we had to attend. I don't know for how long, but in the early thirties my father was Sunday School Superintendent. How that came about or what it meant is an unsolved mystery for me. Dad had been raised Roman Catholic. Our connection with Trinity Church was because of my mother's background. There was nothing at home to indicate that being Sunday School Superintendent had any particular meaning for dad. Very early along the way, thee grew in me strong negative feeling about that part of our lives. There is a vivid memory of a Sunday in spring, the windows were open during the services, the maple trees outside just beginning to get their leaves, the congregation kneeling, and me wanting to be outside so strongly it was almost a visceral pain. Another memory from Holy Week one year; I was walking along High Street and I was thinking, "If there is anything to what was said about Jesus, on that day we called 'Good Friday' there would be storms, and earthquakes, and all manner of disasters because of what people had done to Jesus, and then on Easter the day would dawn warm and gentle, with flowers blooming and birds singing to honor what God had done in response." That may be the faulty reasoning of a child, but even now I wistfully think it would be nice to have that kind of clue.

My mother wasn't involved in the Church, and one Sunday after services when I had gotten to an age that I dared to question things, I asked her,

"How come I have to go to church and you don't?"

She replied, "I have a husband and five children for whom to prepare dinner." (Brian came on the scene February 22, 1934 during a blizzard) "Besides, church will never hurt you." I don't know how others feel about such things, but because something wasn't going to hurt me didn't therefore mean it was worth doing. So somewhere along the way I concluded that the church was for older people who thought they were close to dying, and for children whose parents made them do such things. I further decided that when I could make the choice, I would have nothing to do with the church.

Since he was going to be a fighter, Junior was with dad more than the rest of us. From where I was, it seemed as though they had a good relationship. One Sunday I remember the two of them starting to leave the yard, going to the baseball game probably,

A feeling of loneliness swept over me, and I began to cry. My father turned, and flipped a twenty-five cent coin to me, as though that would take care of anything that could be troubling me.

As time went on, dad just seemed to ignore us. Quite often he was gone on his days off from work. That was never a topic of conversation, either with mom, or with each other. There was no feeling of being close to the others on my part, no sense that anyone cared what I thought or felt. By the time I was in the eighth grade, Junior had quit school, and was working in Hartford at the Heublein Hotel washing dishes. I envied him. It appeared to me as though when a person was working he was independent with nobody telling him what to do. Little did I know at the time.

One Saturday morning in early spring, my mother and father were in the kitchen having an argument. I was in the living room reading a book, which I often did as a means of escape. I was aware that my father began to take his clothes, and load them in his car in preparation for moving out. I just kept reading. Finally dad looked into the living room and said, "Well, so long kid." It's the kind of thing that one would say if there were a good relationship, and you were going to miss that person. It's the kind of thing that my dad would say to me if we had the kind of relationship that I had longed for. Out of regret for that non-relationship I began to weep. Mom heard me and ran out to the car and asked dad not to leave since I was crying. There was no way for me to say, "No! His leaving isn't why I am crying. That he has never been here is what makes me sad." So dad brought his clothes back into the house. The non-relationship continued.

Not long after that, I walked into the house one day, and dad was cutting Junior's hair in the kitchen. As I walked by, dad said to Junior, "If it wasn't for him I would be long gone." I clamped my mouth shut, wanting to say something like, "you son of a bitch, I would be so glad if you were gone." But that would have taken far more courage than I had. I was very afraid of him. He never physically abused me. There is a memory of one spanking only. I am confident I deserved it, and it wasn't cruel. But I feared him. It is the one emotion I have that is related to the memory of the man.

Later that spring he just left. Nothing was ever said to confirm that. He just wasn't around, and nothing about that was ever mentioned. For whatever reasons, I never mentioned that to any of my friends at school.

One of the highlights each year in the village was the Memorial Day celebration. It was a school holiday. There was a big parade in the morning made up of the Boys' Band, men from the American Legion, the Red Men's Lodge, Boy and Girl Scouts.

The parade ended in the cemetery near the WW 1 monument. In those years I thought that everyone from town was present. All the veterans' graves had a new flag and flowers on them. As part of the ceremony, an eighth grade student recited the poem, "In Flanders Field", and another student gave the response. The ceremony always concluded with a bugler playing "Taps" where we were gathered, and from high on the hill at the top part of the cemetery, hidden from view, and muted like an echo, another bugler then answered with "Taps". It was very impressive!

Well, this year I had been chosen by Mrs. MacMasters to recite "In Flanders Fields", and my friend Johnny Danila was to give the response. An added excitement that year was the news of automobile races to be held on Memorial Day afternoon at Cherry Park in Canton for the first time in memory. I hope not to confuse you, but I may do so in adding here that the village of Collinsville is part of the town of Canton. When those of us who lived in the village spoke of Canton, we were referring to a place two miles away where there was a public golf course, Cherry Park, the 1776 summer theater, and two or three small stores. As you can readily imagine, from the middle of May on, there was a great deal of schoolyard talk centered in seeing those races. Much to my dismay, several days before Memorial Day someone decided the parade, and ceremonies at the cemetery would take place in the early afternoon. In my memory they had always been held in the morning.

The other fellows let Johnny and I know that they were sure glad they didn't have to take part in the ceremony, and would be able to get to the races when they began. Johnnie and I both said just as loudly that it wasn't our fault the time had been changed and we were going to the races. Mrs McMasters, of course, heard of this. We intended that she would. She took Johnny and I to the Cloak Room where teacher student conferences tended to be held, and told us that she surely understood how we felt, but that we had made a commitment, and she expected us to do the honorable thing. Mrs. McMasters was someone we liked. Reluctantly we both affirmed that we would do what we had promised. I fully intended to.

Memorial Day dawned bright and beautiful in the way spring can be in New England. Even though we had agreed to take part in the ceremonies at the cemetery, doesn't mean that I didn't feel hard done by. Mid-morning I noticed my mother ironing my Boy Scout suit. I hadn't been active in the Boy Scouts for quite a while. Fearing I knew the answer, I asked my mother why she was ironing the uniform? She replied that she wanted me to wear it because it would look good for the ceremony. I quickly pointed out that I was no longer an active Boy Scout, Johnny Danila wouldn't be wearing a uniform, and we both planned to hitch hike to Cherry Park right afterward, and I sure didn't want to be wearing a Boy Scout uniform at the races. Mom was adamant. I don't think she ever changed her mind when it was made up. In anger I went out of the house, slamming the screen door as I left, went down to Maple Avenue, and hitch hiked to Cherry Park. Johnny Danila arrived not long after the races had begun. He told me that MaCa (the nickname for Mrs. MacMasters) had given him a quarter, and a ride to the races, and that I was in deep trouble. I guess it shouldn't be surprising, but I did not enjoy my first experience of automobile races. (Not only so, I have never cared for automobile races since.) After they were finished, reluctant to return home and face the music, I hitch hiked to Hartford, and found where Junior had a room on Sumner Street. He was working when I got there, but the people said he would be home soon. When he arrived he was understandably surprised to see me. I didn't want to tell him what happened, so I said that dad had left home, and I didn't want to be a burden so I had run away. He replied that I could sleep on the floor in his room, but that if I didn't head for home in the morning he would kick my a__.

The next morning, I went out and began to hitch hike toward Collinsville. A panel truck advertising "Made Rite Buy Rite" bleach picked me up. The young man who was driving was a friendly fellow. He naturally wondered where I was from, and why I wasn't in school. Feeling somewhat sorry for myself, and with some tears, I continued the story of my father leaving home, and me not wanting to be a burden with there being two smaller kids and all, so I had run away. He said something along the line of how much added worry I must be causing my mother, and that he was spending the day selling in Winsted, and that he would be glad to have me along with him. He added that we would have lunch together, and after he finished his work he would drop me off in Collinsville. That meant he would be going to the trouble of driving about four miles out of his way. Spending the day with him was appealing. It gave me several hours respite, so I agreed. When it was time for lunch we went into a grocery store, and he bought some cold cuts, bread, and soda to drink.

We parked by a lake at a city park, and he made us sandwiches. I hadn't eaten since breakfast the day before, so you can well imagine what a treat that was! It was early evening when he drove down River Road, and let me off by Nelson's Gas Station, then turned up Maple Avenue on the way back to Hartford. As I was walking up Main Hill a lady asked me if my brother had come home yet. I told her that I didn't know because I hadn't been home. She said, "Oh, it must have been you that was missing." When I got home, Junior was there, and mom, and Pat, and Brian were sitting outside. I have no memory of what was said.

The next day I went to school, of course. Maca told me that I would have to stay in at recess for the rest of the school year as punishment for what I had done. That was two weeks away. Before the two weeks were up, after the others had gone out for recess one morning, Maca asked me to come to her desk. When I did, she told me that she had heard about my father leaving home, and that she was sorry, and understood now why I had run away, and that I could go out for recess. As I went outside, my thought was that my father leaving had nothing to do with why I ran away, but I sure wasn't going to tell her that. Reflecting upon that it occurs to me that if my father had been on the scene I wouldn't have had the nerve to do what I did. With him gone, a major restraint was lifted from the way I thought about things.

I caddied at the Avon Country Club that summer, beginning as a B Caddy, which paid 75 cents for 18 holes. On most days there were enough golfers so that some of the time I'd get out twice. On weekends it wasn't unusual to go three rounds. When I got home if I had earned $1.75 I'd hold out the money to my mother, $1 in one hand, and 75 cents in the other, and ask her which she wanted. She always took the larger amount, which was no surprise because she really needed the money. I felt good about helping out. Joan had graduated from high school, and was working in West Hartford as a live in helper to a family there. Her salary would have been small, and I have no idea if she sent any home. Junior quit his job at the hotel, and moved back home. He got a job at the Canton Springs Soda Company. I have no way of knowing what arrangement he made with my mother. He maintains that he turned over all but 50 cents each week. He and two of his friends, Phil Picolo and Vita Danila, joined the Naval Reserve in order to add to their income. Junior and I did not have any relationship to speak of in that period. He was four years older, and went his way with his friends. Our paths didn't cross very much except that we slept in the same bed.

From that point on I bought what clothes I had. There is a memory of hitch hiking into Hartford before beginning high school that autumn. I wanted to have new clothes to mark the occasion. I got there a short while before the stores opened, and as I walked along Main Street past Woolworth's, from an open door came the sound of Glenn Miller's "Sunrise Serenade". It was beautiful. I did my shopping in Woolworth's, and bought a pair of slacks, and a sweatshirt. I wasn't exactly a fashion plate as I entered high school, but during those depression years I often was wearing hand me downs from Junior, and this was a step up from that. Oh, there is one more thing to mention about that summer. All the men I knew smoked, and I desperately wanted to be grown-up. I began smoking cigarettes.

There isn't much to tell about high school and I, except that I didn't want to be there. What I wanted was to be able to earn money. That represented to me, not having people tell me what to do anymore. It is, of course, a misapprehension of reality, but it is the way life appeared to me. I didn't do very well in my classes, doing only enough just to get by. I never talked with anyone about how I felt. I recall one day in the class on American History, Miss Finger, the teacher said to me, "Why don't you try? You could be one of my best students." I didn't answer.

Somehow I got through the school year, and caddied again that summer. Junior and his friends in the Naval reserve were called to active duty. He took out a dependency allotment to help out at home. He paid $25 of his monthly salary, and the government added $25. That was $50 a month coming in to my mother. Half of what I earned at the golf course was added to that. Joan had moved back home, and was working at Myrtle Mills in Unionville, five miles away. I don't know what arrangement she had with mom. When August came, I began to dread the coming school year.

The tavern and candy store I mentioned earlier, was owned by Christie Tolides. He had closed down the tavern, and expanded the candy and ice cream fountain. It was referred to by the town's people as the "Greek's", as in "I am going over to the Greek's to get an ice cream cone." Christie also owned a jukebox and pinball machine business. Many stores and restaurants in the neighboring towns had a jukebox or pinball machine, or both. There were times when I was hanging around that Christie would ask me if I wanted to go with him when he was servicing the machines. That August when I was with him, when we passed a sign on the side of the road that said something about a school zone, I'd get a sinking feeling in my stomach, knowing that soon I would have to go back to high school. The law required that I attend until I was 16. As the starting date drew close, I got more desperate. One evening I was talking with Buddy Smith, a classmate since the first grade, and I suggested that we run away from home rather than have to begin classes again. He was all for it. So the day before school was to begin, we headed for Springfield, Massachusetts. I knew someone there who had once been a Barber in Collinsville.

Springfield was to be just a stop along the way in order to see Jimmy Roberts, at whose Barber Shop I had shined shoes during the winter months, when his shop was in town. We were headed for Dearborn, Michigan. In a copy of Liberty Magazine I had read an article about the Henry Ford Trade School at which orphaned boys could learn a trade. When we arrived in Springfield, we found Jimmy's new Barber Shop, told him what we were doing, and where we were headed.

I have no accurate memory of the passage of time during that venture. We got rides as far as Albany, New York, then walked a long way through the city to where the highway went west. Buddy had some money, and I remember stopping at a White Castle for a bag of burgers. I think they were ten for a dollar, but memory could easily be faulty on that. We tried to hitch a ride, but unsuccessfully. Hours went by, and we were both exhausted. Finally, we decided to head back to Springfield. We got rides with truck drivers, and arrived late the next day. We went to Jimmy's place, and after he closed for the day, He and a friend of his, Bob Reuter, helped us find a room in downtown Springfield. I should add, Jimmie Roberts had introduced Bob and my sister Joan, and they were dating.

The next day, Buddy and I went to a local golf course and caddied. Since school was in session we were the only caddies there. We both made some money, but I have no memory of how much. On the way to our room we stopped at Jimmy's shop. Feeling grown-up and able to choose now, we asked Jimmie if he would get us a bottle of Muscatel, which he agreed to do. I've done many stupid things in my life. Getting that bottle of wine, and the two of us drinking it is just one of those things. We hadn't been eating well. Needless to say, I became very sick. I threw up meals that were just a memory.

I don't recall now exactly how many days we were away from home. It was 1940, and jobs for people our age were not plentiful. We thought about trying to join the CCC, but without parents to sign for us ruled that out. Winter was not that far away, so we finally decided to go back home. We arrived in the evening and no one was home when I got there. I fell asleep on the porch where I slept in the summertime. I was wakened by mom, who said, "So you've come back home." I was exhausted, and went right back to sleep.

The next day, I had to go to school. When I arrived, Mr. Bowdoin, the principal, called me into his office. He didn't have much to say; just "I'm through fooling around with you. The next time you miss school I am going to turn you over to the Juvenile Court." So, there I was, present in body because that's what the law required. I didn't do any of the homework, didn't participate in the classroom. I hated every moment of it. Finally, in early December I went to Mr. Bowdoin, and told him that things were difficult at home, and it would help if I could get a job. He replied that Connecticut law made it impossible for me to get a job on any kind of machinery until the age of 16, and that farm, or work in a store or restaurant was about all that was permitted. He added that there weren't many stores or restaurants that would hire someone my age when so many people were out of work. He encouraged me to give it a try, and to let him know how things went. Something sad about this whole thing is that I was just trying to get away from school. My getting a job seemed impossible, and I did not even try.

Each weekday morning I'd get up and have breakfast as if I was going to school. Then I would go down town, and spend the morning hanging around "Leo's Lunch". At noon I'd go home for lunch as I did on a school day. Afternoons I'd spend in the Bowling Alley. When I think about that, it was a grim way to live. At the time it was preferable to school. One day in the middle of January, Leo, the owner of the lunch and poolroom told me that a Truant Officer from Hartford had been looking for me. Not many days later on the way home to lunch, as I was walking up Main Hill with the boys who lived across the street, Benny asked me if my mother knew I wasn't going to school. When I said that she didn't, he replied, "She's going to now. I have a letter for her from "Tweak" (the nickname for Mr Bowdoin). I wanted Benny to give me the letter, but of course he couldn't do that. When mom read the note, she sat down and cried. I went back to school that afternoon. Mr. Bowdoin never said anything to me again. There is a memory of several of us out on the fire escape sneaking a smoke. Mr Bowdoin came around the corner, and told the others to go to his office, but not me. Not surprising, he had given up on me as worth the trouble. Later on in spring I got a job at a tobacco farm in Simsbury, and dropped out of school and nothing was said.

Thus began a year and a half of bouncing from one job to another. Sammy Gauthier quit his job at Bristol's dairy farm to go to work delivering groceries for

Randall's, one of the grocery stores on Main Street. He suggested that I go ask Mr. Bristol for his old job. I was hired. Mr. Bristol had 22 dairy cows, and a milk route in Collinsville. He sold milk to his customers for 14 cents a quart. Our day began at 5 AM. He had a hired man who fed the cows, milked them, and did other work on the farm. First thing in the morning I'd load the milk truck, then after breakfast we did the milk route. That took until about 1 o'clock. After the noon meal, which in those days was called dinner, I washed the bottles, and then filled them with the morning's milk, using a ten quart can. This took most of the afternoon. Then I'd go to where the cows were pastured, and drive them to the barn, put them in their stanchions, and give them their feed. The other hired man would arrive and help me. Then we would begin milking the cows, using a portable milking machine that did two cows at a time. The milk was poured by hand through a strainer into the milk cans. When the first one was filled, I'd take it to the milk room, strain it again, fill the rest of the bottles for the milk route, and then put them in racks, and store them in the cooler. By then it was around 6:30 and time for supper. I received $10 a week, and room and board. Also, I had Sunday off from after the noon meal until 5 o'clock the next morning.

Mrs. Bristol was a substitute teacher for the grammar school, and she was a very good cook. Mr. and Mrs. Bristol were fine people. They had one child, a son Eddy, who was a couple of years younger than me. Sometimes he and I would go across the road, and swim in the river before going to bed. Later in the summer when the corn was growing well, Mr. Bristol asked if I would be willing to drive the tractor while he, and two fellows from town did the cultivating. I really enjoyed driving an automobile when the opportunity presented itself. In that period I would have followed someone around like a puppy dog if they just allowed me to drive their car when we were going somewhere. So I happily agreed to drive the tractor. It wasn't an automobile, but it was the next best thing. The three cultivators were attached to a bar on the back of the tractor, and in this manner three rows of corn were cultivated at a time. We worked until long after dark, and by the time I'd get the tractor back to the barn, it was close to ten o'clock. That meant 5 AM arrived swiftly. So it was that the days and weeks passed. Mr. Bristol didn't say very much. He never said anything about my work. I know now in a way I didn't then that my spirit craved praise. I didn't know anything about love, but I knew a great deal about how approval felt. Just as surely, when there was disapproval in whatever form, I was frightened. All that got twisted in me in such a way such that in the absence of Mr. Bristol's approval, I felt that he didn't like me. So I decided to get away from what was uncomfortable for me by quitting. To compound the problem, I was afraid to tell him I was quitting for fear it would lead to him saying harsh things. So one Sunday after dinner, I left for town, and didn't go back.

The next job was at a gas station. It was a small Texaco station about three miles from town on the way to Unionville. George Chartier, Nelson's older brother, and his neighbor, Harold parent owned the dealership of the station. Harold had been a classmate of mine. He was a silent partner, and it was George who hired me. I was the daytime attendant, and that meant I opened the station, spent the day there, and George would relieve me around 5 o'clock after he got off work at the Collins Company. My pay was $12 a week. I had Sunday off. It was a very boring job. There weren't many customers, and sometimes while sitting inside I'd fall asleep. At the end of the fifth week, George told me not come in on Monday.

Then I went to work for Leo Bachand at his Lunch-Pool Room. This was where many of the town's single men spent their evenings, or at least part of them. In one room was the restaurant with a pinball machine, and a jukebox. In the other room were two pool tables, some chairs where several

Of the fellows could sit and watch the pool shooters, and two rest rooms. In one corner there was a table for playing cards. Leo paid me $10 a week, and two meals each day. During this period when I was earning money, I gave my mother half of my weekly pay. Joan had married Bob, and was living in Springfield. Mom had a day job in the neighborhood taking care of a child while the parents worked. Between what she earned, Junior's allotment, and the $5 a week I gave her, she managed.

In using the term 'restaurant' to describe one room, gives the wrong impression. The name of the place was, "Leo's Lunch". It was a place where one could get a good sandwich, a piece of pie and a cup of coffee. There were two or three short order meals available. A meal of hamburger steak, potatoes, and another vegetable cost 40 cents, a piece of pie 10 cents, and a cup of coffee 5 cents. Each weekday Leo prepared a hot meal for regular customers who came from the Collins Company during the lunch hour. I served ten to fifteen customers, all males. Leo's was a men's hang out. The only time I ever saw a woman in there was if someone's husband was playing cards when he should have been home, and she came to fetch him. That happened once or twice while I worked there, and it was not a pleasant scene.

My day began at 9:00 AM. Waiting on customers, peeling potatoes, helping Leo get ready for the noon meal was my job. After lunch I ate, then did the dishes, and had the afternoons off. Then I returned to work at 4:30. Now and then Leo took his family to the movies, and I took care of business until he got back. The place didn't close until around 3 AM, and most nights I stayed until then. Leo was a good boss. I liked him and I think he liked me.

That December (1941) Pearl Harbor was attacked. Charlie Konopka joined the Marines two weeks later. He was a good friend. I wished that I was old enough to join with him, but wishing didn't help. Several weeks later he sent a post card to the gang at Leo's in which he said, "Tell Soucy that if he joins the Marines they will make a man out of him or ship back the pieces". At Christmas, mom, Pat, and Brian went by bus to Springfield to be with Joan, Bob, and their first child, David. Mom wanted me to go, too. I said that I would hitch hike up later, but had no intention of doing so. It was a miserable Christmas. I should say here, Christmas had always been a big day in our life as a family. No matter how poor we were, each one of us received several presents. Maybe they were something to wear, but they were ours, and they were personal. Thanksgiving and Christmas were the two times during the year that we used the Dining Room. There was a big roasting chicken that we always bought from Mrs. Sydlo. The meal had all of the holiday fixings. Mom made fruit cake, and a Christmas pudding that each of the children would have to stir while making a wish. Each of the older children was allowed a tiny glass of port wine. Those Christmas celebrations were a grand part of our childhood. This one was different, Junior in the Navy, mom and the kids at Joan's, me home alone. Leo's closed earlier that night. With some of the fellows, I went to a midnight movie there in town, walked home around daybreak, and slept all day. Even as I write about it, I feel lonely.

Joan, with her baby came by bus for a visit. She was expecting their second child, so knew that soon visits would not be possible. While with us she asked if I would come and live with them. Since she was pregnant she said that I could be quite a help to them, such as staying with David of an evening while they went to a movie now and then. She added that I would be able to find a job in the city, and that I wouldn't have to pay them anything, and could still send money to help at home. I was tired from the job at Leo's. Long hours every day, and I hadn't had a day off since beginning three months earlier. So I agreed to go back with Joan. I told Leo that my sister needed me. It was a good excuse so I didn't mind telling him I was quitting.

The three of us rode back to Springfield on the bus. On the way, Joan told me that a cousin of Bob's named Tom was staying with them a little while. Tom was in the process of joining the Marines, and while he was there we would have to share a convertible bed in their Living Room. That was no problem for me. Tom was a few years older than me, and we got along fine. I envied him being able to enlist. I had my birth certificate with me so that I could show it to any potential employer. During that period, while Tom was in the process of joining the Marines, I decided to try and alter my birth certificate so that I would be able to enlist in the Navy. Changing 1925 to 1923 seemed fairly easy. When I had done it as well as I could, I went down to the Navy Recruiting Office. I don't recall now if the Recruiter was a Chief or an Ensign, but my attempt at forgery didn't fool him. He said that he could sure understand my desire to enlist, but if I did it under false pretences, and that was later discovered, I'd be kicked out, and maybe not allowed to get back in. He added that it was only a few months until September when I would be old enough. So I began to search seriously for a job.

I was hired at the first place I applied, a small drug store downtown. Mr. Markell, owned two drug stores, one in a neighboring town that he managed, and this one managed by the Pharmacist, with me to assist. I was paid $14 a week. It was interesting for a while, but that soon wore off, and I began to pine for Collinsville. That was accentuated one weekend when four of the fellows came for a visit. I was on duty at the store, and was surprised to see them when they entered. They asked if I knew of any place in the city where they could get a tire or two. With rationing on, tires were becoming scarce. I asked the Pharmacist if he knew of any possibilities, and he told me of a gas station owner who maybe could help. He gave me a couple of hours off to go with my friends to see. It was a time, however when if someone had tires they hoarded them for friends, and our quest that day was fruitless. Seeing my friends, however, increased my longing to be back home in Collinsville. That week I decided to return. I didn't have whatever it would have taken to tell Mr. Markell I was leaving. After he paid me on Saturday, I just left and never went back. Nor did I have what it would have taken to tell Joan I was going home. I made the preparations, bought my bus ticket, and the night before I was leaving, while Joan and Bob were at the movie, I took my few articles of clothing from a drawer they had given me to use in their dresser, put them in my small suitcase and placed it in back of the door in the Living Room.

My plan was to get up early and leave before they got up in the morning. Then I began to worry about one of them opening my drawer, and seeing nothing in it. I could only imagine that happening by accident, and had the brilliant thought that if either of them tried to open the drawer, and it happened to stick they would give up and go to bed. So I got a hammer and a finishing nail, and nailed the drawer shut. I then went to bed and was sleeping by the time they got home. I have no idea why Bob tried to open that drawer. As you can readily guess, he was furious when he saw what I had done. That was a beautiful piece of their bedroom furniture into which I had driven that nail. Standing in front of him with my heart pounding while he shouted at me is as if it happened yesterday. It was a relief to leave the next morning before they got up. I am guessing that Bob and Joan were just as relieved to have me leave.

It was good to be back home.

Harold Parent was working in the Shipping Department of the Hartford Spinning Company in Unionville. He asked me if I would be interested in working with him. I was hired, and my pay was 50 cents an hour, far more than I had earned on any previous job. It was summer now, and soon I would be old enough to enlist.

In August, Alex Gatska, one of the pool room crowd, asked me to go to Hartford with him and join the Navy. By then my efforts to change the date on my birth certificate had resulted in a far better appearance. However, remembering what the Recruiting Officer in Springfield told me, it seemed much wiser not to lie. When I went with Alex, I told the man I would be 17 on September 1st.

He replied that a physical exam was good only for ten days, and that if I came in on August 22, and passed the exam, the Navy would give me a birthday present. Alex passed his physical that day, and left for Boot Camp only a few days later. I was envious. In back of all this was the underlying fear that I wouldn't be able to pass the physical exam.

I had always been very thin, and in no way did I resemble the husky sailor portrayed in the Recruiting Posters walking up the gangplank of a cruiser with his sea bag on his shoulder. By then I didn't like the job at the spinning factory. So I stopped reporting for work. I took a temporary job at an apple orchard until it was time for my physical. I was part of crew hired to cut the weeds and tall grass in the orchard. Using scythes, we worked through the day. In the morning when we began it was wet, and some of the weeds were poison ivy. Above each ankle I developed a red band of blistering skin. I didn't scratch it because I didn't want it to get worse for when I was to take that physical. When I reported, on the 22nd, to the recruiting office in the Post Office building in Hartford, the first thing the doctor asked was about the red inflammation above each ankle. He readily understood, of course, when I told him. Toward the end of the physical he told me to pee in a jar they had there. The room was full of doctors, pharmacist mates, and others trying to enlist. There was no way I could put anything in that jar. He suggested that I go for a walk around the block and then try again. Same result! He said,

"There's no way I can keep the recruiting office open until you manage to pee in the jar. You'll have to come back in tomorrow."

That evening, while hanging around at Leo's I made sure to drink a lot of water, and even went up to Dr. Cox's office and had him check my urine. He said it was clear as water and tested fine. The next morning I didn't empty my bladder, or stop to eat any breakfast. I went right down to Maple Avenue, and began hitch hiking to Hartford. When I got to the recruiting office, I really had to go, filled up the jar they gave me, and asked where the toilet was. When I got back he told me that I had passed the physical, and would report to New Haven to be sworn in on my birthday. At that moment I was probably the happiest 17 year old in the whole land. When speaking of being happy, there is something that needs to be added.

Throughout this period of my life I had a major interest in girls. That interest was buried by lack of transportation, little money, and very little self-confidence. I did tell Gertrude Goodrich that I liked her, but she let me know that a high school classmate, Randall Bentley, was her boyfriend. So much for this teenager's early romance.

When I got outside the post office after passing the physical exam, I placed one foot on the front bumper of a parked car, took the cuff of my trouser leg in each hand, and gave that poison oak a good scratching. Then I hitched a ride back home to tell my mother the good news. She said,

"I wish I had ten boys to send." After a bite to eat, I headed down to Leo's to tell whoever was there. They, of course, all knew that I was trying to enlist. On the way, down by the library, a fellow in his thirties nicknamed "Birdie" was coming in the other direction.

"How did you make out?" he asked. With a happy grin, I joyously replied,

"I passed."

"You're going to spend the war in the brig," was his response.

Nothing, however, could diminish the glad feeling in me. I had passed a test and would be doing a man's job. A small write-up appeared in the Hartford Courant saying that I was the youngest recruit to enlist at the Hartford Depot up to that time. Naturally, I felt proud of that distinction.

The days went by rapidly. Mom and I had to go before a Notary Public to witness when she signed the enlistment papers. A neighbor who was dating her drove me to Hartford to catch the train to New Haven. With a group of other recruits I took the oath. There is no memory of what we were promising that day, but whatever it was I meant it. When we were boarding the train to go to Providence, Rhode Island, a Chief Petty Officer said to me,

"Happy Birthday." I felt tall.

2

The Navy Years

As you can imagine, it is not an exaggeration to say that the Navy years began on a high note. When we arrived in Providence, a Navy truck was waiting to take us to Newport Naval Training Station for our four weeks of Boot Camp. During peacetime that training took three months, but the demands of a rapidly expanding Navy had shortened the training period. When we entered the gate, the Boots along the streets shouted, "You'll be sorry!" as we passed. The events during the rest of the day are a jumble. We received another physical examination in a large room filled with naked bodies, and doctors, and pharmacist mates. As we moved along someone made marks on us with mercurochrome, and finally I was sent into a room with a Psychiatrist seated at his desk. I stood there before him as naked as the day I was born while he looked through some papers, obviously about me. He finally looked up and asked,

"How old are you?"

For the past year I had been saying, "Sixteen" when asked. From force of habit I began, "Six…", but then said "Seventeen Sir". Standing before him, five feet ten inches tall, and weighing 121 pounds, I probably looked around fourteen. He smiled and said,

"That will be all. Good luck."

We were issued a seabag, a hammock and mattress, uniforms, dungarees, underwear, towels, soap, tooth paste and a brush, ankle boots, and shoe shine gear. Our civilian clothes we left to be shipped home. We were taken to our barracks on the second floor of a building where we were to live for the next month. Since it was getting late we were marched over to the mess hall for the evening meal. By the time we got back to the barracks it was time for Taps. We made up our bunks, and crawled in shortly after lights out. From nervousness, I guess, there was joking back and forth. Wishing to be part of the crowd, trying to sound like Lou Costello, I said,

"I'm a bad boy!' There was laughter, and then the angry sound of a chief who had just entered the room.

"Who said that," he roared? No one responded. He came down to our end of the barracks, and to our side of the room,

"You on this side, hit the deck." When we were standing he said,

"Unless the one who said that owns up to it, you will all get dressed, and with sea bags on your shoulders report to the drill field." Naturally unwilling to be the reason for that, I said,

"I did it."

"Get dressed and report to the Officer of the Deck." Said the chief. "We just might send you back home." I had no idea what the Officer of the Deck was, or where such a person could be found. Feeling badly, I got dressed as quietly as I could, went downstairs and outside. I saw a sailor standing guard over by the clothes line, so I went and asked where I could find the Officer of the Deck. He whispered,

"I'll get in trouble if I am seen talking to anyone." He then told me where the drill hall was where the Officer of the Deck had his desk.

It wasn't far, and when I walked in there were several people doing various things. I asked one of them where I could find the Officer of the Deck? He directed me to a chief who was at a desk talking to a sailor. When he got to me, I explained that I had been sent to him because of talking after lights out. He asked what company I belonged to. It is a wonder I knew. When I told him, he asked,

"You just got in this afternoon didn't you?" I affirmed that was true.

"Go back and hit the sack", he said with a hint of a smile.

"You are going to need your rest. And just remember, no talking after lights out." The weight of the world was lifted from my shoulders. Thanks chief, wherever you are, for your understanding.

Boot Camp was like a door opening on a new world. The chief who was assigned to us had been in the Navy for more than twenty years. Originally from Georgia, the south flavored his thinking, and enriched his speaking. I don't remember his name, but something of his instruction is as real as if it happened yesterday. What a formidable task he had. Taking a large group of civilians, ranging in age from seventeen to thirty, from different backgrounds, molding us into a military unit, sailors ready to go to sea. The chief had a ready sense of humor. Early on, with us assembled outside the barracks he said,

"When I call you out heah, I mean business. I don't want any skylarking! You know what skylarking is? That's grab ass. When ah says 'attention' ah mean ATTENTION. Even if a snake crawls up yo ass you leave it dayah." In that vein the days went by.

Reveille was at 5 A.M. An instructor younger than our Chief led us on a two mile run. That was difficult for me. I had already been smoking cigarettes for over two years. Also, I hadn't been eating regular meals some of that time. But we ran, with me much closer to the end of the pack. We marched and did calisthenics. We were vaccinated and inoculated following which, seabag inspection was held. We learned how to stencil our clothes, and wash them, and when they were dry, how to pack them into a seabag. We had many different kinds of drills ranging from the use of gas masks in a room where tear gas was released, to self-defense. One afternoon the whole company was marched to a dental clinic. The dentist to whom I was assigned was a young man. As he talked with his assistant it was evident he had been drafted right after he graduated. The bitterness he felt was evident in things he said. What he found in my mouth didn't brighten his day at all. In our family, we had never been taught to care for our teeth. The county nurse visited the school once a year with instructions on brushing after meals. She would then pass out a toothbrush, and a tube of toothpaste to each of the students. At home, we would use it until the toothpaste was gone, and that was the end of tooth care until the nurse came the next year. It came as no surprise that the dentist in Boot Camp found twelve cavities that needed filling. He proceeded to do just that, drilling first, and then filling. By the time he did the last filling, it felt as though the back of my throat was filled with gravel. The dentist said, "Don't bite down." It felt as though I was going to choke. When the dentist turned away, I placed my tongue against the roof of my mouth and tried to swallow. He turned back just as I did that. It must have looked to him as though I bit down, although I don't know how it could. In any case, he vented his anger upon me. It was a major relief to get out of there. My thinking was that it could never be that bad again, and I have never minded going to the dentist since that experience.

When our four weeks of training was completed there was a big ceremony held at the Drill Field. We were given a week of leave. I was a proud and happy 17 year old, walking with shoulders back, sticking out a chest I scarcely had. Taking the bus from Hartford to Collinsville, I could hardly wait. When we pulled up in front of Joe Mac's Drug Store, with my kit in hand, I stepped down to Main Street. Pat Gauthier was going by on his way home from work. Pat was an old French Canadian who lived with his married daughter on Main Hill. His teeth were gone and he chewed snuff. On weekend evenings he often spent time at the Melody Grill drinking beer. Then, as many did, he would come down to Leo[s for a bowl of soup when the bar closed at 2 AM. He didn't try to remember names, called everyone Pat. When he saw me getting off of the bus, he said,

"Is that you, Pat?" I smiled and said,

"Yes it is."

"You don't look any better," was his response. So much for standing tall, and sticking out my chest.

Memories of that leave are rather sketchy. I spent time hanging around Leo's and Christie's, and visited the high school one afternoon. I saw Gertrude, and visited that evening at her house. One late morning I went to a movie in Hartford with Len Pomaski, Ralph Yeske, and the young bartender from the Melody Grill. When the week was up, a neighbor, Kenny Quinion drove me back to the bus station in Hartford. I reported to Sea Unit in Newport, a station from which the graduates of Boot Camp were dispersed throughout the Navy. Sea Unit was not a good place to be. It was commanded by a four striper, who was nicknamed Captain Bligh. Under him were several chiefs who seemed to take a sadistic delight in giving us a bad time. There were times and places where smoking was forbidden. It was said that if Captain Bligh caught a sailor smoking where he should not have been, that he would take the cigarette, and put it out in the sailor's hand. I didn't personally see that happen, but I believe it. I did see the Captain catch a sailor with the top button of his Pea Jacket unbuttoned. The Captain pulled the button from the jacket, and gave it to the sailor, saying,

"When you are sewing this back on, maybe you'll remember to keep it buttoned next time."

As each day went by, sailors with whom we had gone through Boot training would be shipped out. Finally, there were just two of us left, Joel Vodolla and me. Each day we would go to the chaplain's office, and ask his assistant if there was any word on where we were going. He was a prissy kind of a man, probably in his 30s. Joel and I had nicknamed him, "Blinky". Each day, after looking through several sheets of paper, the answer was the same. No word on where we were going.

To provide a little more insight into what it was like at Sea Unit, one night we got back from the movie a little later than usual. Lights were out at 2130, and it was five minutes after Taps. As we prepared to get into our hammocks, the men were talking quietly about the movie, or whatever. In each barracks there was a two-way speaker system. Suddenly an angry voice loudly told us to get into our uniforms, and report outside the barracks in five minutes. When we were assembled outside, a chief strode up and down in front of us telling us what a worthless bunch we were. He said that soon we would be going out to the Big Time, and when we did we would probably be killed, and it would serve us right. He added that he wished that he could take a machine gun, and get it over for us right then. I have no recollection of how long we had to stand out there at attention, but that is something of how Sea Unit was. Joel and I were there way too long. One of us said,

"What if they have lost our records, and we are stuck here for the duration?" Horrible to contemplate! Finally on the 23rd day, Blinky gave us the good news. Joel was headed for Aviation

Mechanic's School, and I was going to the Fleet Sound School. Blinky wouldn't tell our destination. I have no idea why. But he did say,

"Be prepared to wear your whites." That came as good news to me. It was getting close to the end of October, and it was cold there in Newport.

The next day we packed all of our gear, and reported to a railroad siding where all the sailors being shipped out that day were crowded. Joel and I were separated. Sailors were placed in one of six or seven large groups. Each had their sea bags, with bedroll lashed around them. I don't know how much that weighed, but it was just about all I could handle. As we waited, a train would slowly puff it's way onto the siding. When it halted one of the groups were instructed to shoulder their packs, then they would slowly file aboard. This happened several times, and each took quite a while. I could picture our turn to board arriving, and me struggling with the pack on my shoulder, and Captain Bligh pulling me out of line, and having to report back to Sea Unit. Fortunately for me it didn't happen that way. We finally got settled aboard a train, and the petty officer escorting us told us we were headed for Key West, Florida. That was joyful news, and there was an air of excitement. One of the recruits, who turned out to be from upper New York State, began to talk with a southern drawl.

Until I joined the Navy, the sixteen mile trip from Collinsville to Hartford seemed like a long distance away from home. Each year the eighth grade looked forward to the "Hartford Trip". It was something they had been saving for and working toward for four years. Suddenly I was on a train heading for Florida, sleeping in a Pullman Berth at night, and eating in the Dining Car. It was a wow kind of experience for this seventeen years old boot. I can't exaggerate the wonder of Palm Trees, the brilliant white of Florida sand, the warmth of tropic sun. In Miami we left the train and caught a bus for Key West. It was crowded and I gave my seat to a woman traveling with her daughter. Men did that then. It was a little over 150 miles. We had rest stops along the way.

The Naval Base in Key West, after the experience of Sea Unit in Newport, was like going from hell to heaven in my thinking. The uniform of the day was white trousers and Tee shirts. The chiefs were relaxed. What we did at Sound School was enjoyable. Entering the world of anti-submarine warfare, very early our hearing ability was well tested. Then we learned about the equipment used. When this had been mastered we went to sea in small groups on ships equipped with sound gear. There were two old Four Stack destroyers, Dahlgren and Noa, and several Eagle Boats from WWI. Students took turns manning the sound gear as we worked with submarines. The weather was fine, and the sea gentle. Nevertheless, on some days I felt a bit queasy. The Noa and Dahlgren were quite a bit larger than the Eagle Boats, and provided a smoother ride. The five weeks of Sound School went by rapidly. When it concluded we were promoted to Third Class Petty Officers. Here I had been in the Navy for a little over three months, and already I was a Third Class Soundman. Elated, I sent a telegram to my mother with the news. We were told that we could request our next duty station, and they would try to honor our request as assignments were made. A list of what was open to us was posted. One of the possibilities was to stay at the Sound School for a course in maintaining and repairing the Sound Gear. Upon satisfactory completion, promotion to Second Class was awarded. That had no appeal for me. I hadn't enlisted in the Navy to spend my time going to school. Sound men served on small wooden Sub Chasers, a bit larger PC boats made of steel, Destroyer Escorts, and largest of all Destroyers. Having experienced that queasy feeling several times, I knew I wished to be on the largest ship possible. There was no contest, and I applied for Destroyer duty. My request was granted, and I received orders to report to the USS Ringgold in New York. I wasn't all that thrilled to be heading back to where it was cold, but the thought of going aboard a Destroyer was exciting for me.

After making the train trip north, we reported to the Receiving Ship at Pier 92 in the city. They were over crowded, and a group of us were sent to Lido Beach in Long Island where a big luxurious building that had been a Yacht Club had been taken over by the Navy. It was like living in a hotel. There were many sailors waiting to be sent to their next assignment. After formation one morning a group of sailors were talking together. The topic was convoy duty in the North Atlantic. A chief said that if your ship was torpedoed and you had to abandon ship you had about five minutes to live after hitting the water during the winter months. Looking out to sea and seeing the huge, cold waves breaking against the shore, I believed him.

We were at Lido Beach only for a few days. From there we went to Pier 92, also a receiving station. The sleeping quarters were on an upper floor, but we ate our meals in the part of the building at street level. When eating trucks would drive through. Everything was so new to me that I was half scared a good part of the time that I was going to do something wrong, and get into trouble.

December was half over and we had no idea when the Ringgold would be ready. There was liberty, but I never knew what to do. I can recall one night seeing three different movies on Times Square. I felt very alone. We were required to stand watches. Once I had a mid-watch on a Brig Ship named the Camden. I was shut inside the cell where some prisoners were sleeping. They all had shaved heads, and it was a very uncomfortable experience. Another time I stood watch on the hulk of the Normandy. She had rolled over onto her side after catching on fire while being refitted for transporting troops. I think that the watch standing was just something they had us doing. After morning muster one day, a chief addressed us and said that they had just passed a law to begin drafting men into the Navy. He added that they would no longer be kicking sailors out of the Navy with Bad Conduct Discharges for going over the hill, because that's exactly what some of the draftees would want. He said, "From now on they will probably shoot those who go over the hill." I had no intention of going over the hill. I couldn't understand how anyone would deliberately do something like that, and be in that kind of trouble.

Finally the welcome news was given to those of us waiting for the Ringgold that we were to report aboard her at the Brooklyn Navy Yard. I remember how impressed I felt when I first saw her. Until then the only Destroyers I'd seen were the two Four Pipers in Key West. IT was like the difference between a Model A and a new Ford V8. I was assigned a bunk and locker in C Division, the next to the last compartment aft. A second class Quartermaster named Browning was doing the assigning. He and I hit it off right from the beginning, and went on liberty together that night.

The next day was the day before Christmas. Mid-morning we had a commissioning ceremony, and Commander, Thomas F. Conley, Jr. was given command of the Ringgold. After the ceremony those of us whose homes were close enough were given a 48 hour Liberty so that we could be home for Christmas. I remember very little about that Christmas of 1942. What I recall from that period is the strangeness of being aboard ship. During the daytime there were work parties for things like loading stores, and ammunition. Sometimes Browning and I would sneak away from the ship, and go up to the PX when he had word that a work party was about to happen. A Watch, Quarter, and Station, Bill was posted. Each man of the crew thus learned his watch section, where his battle station was, and where he was to muster with his division. Some of us were also assigned to be on Special Sea Detail. That meant we had a particular assignment when the ship was getting underway, or entering port. My Special Sea Detail was to man the Sound gear. IT all was a jumble to me, and I suspect to many others who had never been on a ship before. Being a P.O. 3/c helped, and having Browning for a friend helped a whole lot more.

One day tug boats came, and eased the Ringgold away from the dock. We went and tied up alongside an ammunition barge. The whole day was spent in loading ammunition. Cans of 20mm and 40mm for the machine guns, and five inch shells and cans of powder for the 5 inch guns. When we finished, tug-boats took us back dockside. After the hard day of work I had the mid-watch on the bridge until 4 A.M. It seemed as though I'd just gotten to sleep when the loud speaker called the Special Sea Detail to go to stations. I was as sure as could be that whatever it was, it didn't apply to me. Surely no one would expect someone who had just gotten off watch to get out of the bunk, and do something else. I went back to sleep immediately. The next I knew Whaley, a first class Quartermaster was saying, "Soucy, the Special Sea Detail was called five minutes ago, and you're supposed to be on the bridge. Now get you're a__ up there." I still couldn't believe it, but I knew the voice of authority when I heard it. We got underway, and when we got outside the harbor, the Special Sea Detail was secured, and the watch was set. I had the watch along with a Soundman named Warren. The word had been passed that we were headed for Casco Bay for some sea trials. When I got off watch, Whaley came to me in the compartment, and he said, "Soucy, if you weren't a boot you're a_ would be on report. When the Special Sea Detail is called that means you on the Sound gear, and I don't care how tired you are or what watch you just had, you be on that Sound gear." I was continually learning that my hopes, and the Navy's expectations didn't always coincide.

We went through the Cape Cod Canal on our way to Portland, Maine. The water was like glass. I felt pretty salty. There was no liberty in Portland while we were at Casco Bay. We would get underway each morning, and engage in tests and drills during the day. We stood regular watches, and were called to General Quarters for various drills. Then towards evening we would return to Casco Bay for the night. The weather was cold, and the sea was fairly rough. I would feel woozy but I didn't throw up. Some of the sailors were seasick, and it gave me a feeling of being more salty than they were. Nevertheless, it was always a welcome sound when the Special Sea Detail was called because we were headed towards harbor.

Scuttlebutt is a Navy term for rumors. After we'd been working out of Casco Bay for about ten days the Scuttlebutt was that we were heading for Guantanamo Bay, Cuba for our Shakedown cruise. That came as good news because I knew it would be warm there. Surely enough, the next day while still at Special Sea Detail on our way out of the harbor, the Captain announced over the ship's speaker that we were on our way to Cuba.

I had the first watch. It wasn't long until the ship was pitching and rolling much more than anything I had experienced before. The weather was cold, and the wind strong. The chair on which I sat in front of the Sound gear was bolted to the deck. Good thing, because I'd never have been able to echo range in search of submarines otherwise. The Sound gear in front of me, and the stool upon which I sat would rise, and then lean forward as though going down an incline. I began to get a funny feeling at the base of my skull, and a dry taste in the back of my mouth. It was a relief when I was relieved at 0800. When I got down onto the main deck, the rough seas were awesome. The Destroyer traveling with us would disappear from sight, and then appear again as we topped another wave. I don't mean to imply that I was standing there enjoying the scenery. What I was doing was throwing up as I made my way aft, headed for my bunk. The Head was well occupied by other sailors being sea sick as I entered the hatch, and went below to C Division. The men off watch were in their bunks. I didn't even take off my shoes, just crawled in and lay on my stomach. After a while I began to feel better. Three and a half hours later when the word was passed that chow was being served, Pete Brown, a Quartermaster who wasn't sick asked if I would like for him to bring me back a sandwich. By then I was beginning to feel hungry, and when he came back with a large sandwich made with corned beef hash, it tasted very good. Not long after I went on watch at 1600 I was sick again. There was a bucket out on the signal bridge for that purpose. I put it to good use, so much for being salty.

The seond day out the sea was rougher if possible, and the cold had formed ice on all the rigging. At mealtime only sandwiches and coffee were being served in the mess hall. I didn't try to eat before going on watch. Maybe I should have, because when I got sick I'd have had something to throw. As it was I'd come running out of the Charthouse where the Sound gear was, and stand over the bucket dry heaving. Stephens, the Signalman on watch, laughed. He thought that me retching over the bucket was hilarious. Once he said,

"If you taste anything round and brown, Souce, swallow hard because you're turning inside out." For some reason I couldn't see the humor in that at the moment.

There was no consolation in it, but more than half the crew was seasick. Even sailors who had been in the Navy for some time, and sailed on larger vessels were among those of us not keeping anything down. By the time we got to Cape Hatteras the weather got warmer, and I was no longer nauseated. The moon was full at night, and I remember the Chief Pharmacist's Mate saying

"That's a Carolina moon."

No matter how sick we felt we still stood our regular watches, four hours on and eight off. In addition, there were morning and evening battle stations for an hour. During the daylight hours we were often called to battle stations for one drill or another. The Captain said to the Officer of the Deck,

"Sick or not they've got to get used to it."

As you would imagine it was a pleasure to get to the Caribbean Sea. It was warm, and the sea was calm. Most of those who had been sick were now looking chipper, and showing up for meals. We operated out of Guantanamo for three weeks. Everything that could be tested on the ship was put through its test. We made 44.7 knots during speed trials. That's 2,130 tons cutting through the water at close to 50 miles an hour. I began to feel proud of being a Destroyer sailor.

Lt. Cmdr. S.A. McCornock was our Executive Officer. The crew called him Sam because of his initials, but not to his face, of course.

I was fascinated by messages sent between ships by a flashing light using Morse code. One day I asked Mr. McCornock if I could become a Signalman. He replied that he wanted me to go to Materiel School, and learn to repair the sound gear when it broke down. I told him that I wasn't really interested in learning how to repair the Sound gear, but that I did want to be a Signalman. Something else going on inside me was the fact that other sailors referred to Soundmen as 'ping girls", and that was a very negative thing, of course. The Exec wasn't open to the idea of me changing from Soundman to Signalman, much to my disappointment.

When our Shakedown was completed we headed up the East Coast to New York. As we made our way through the Windward Passage the wind picked up and the sea became choppy. It wasn't long, and I was seasick again. However, it didn't last anywhere nearly as long as on the trip down to Cuba. I wasn't feeling real robust, but things were better. I even was able to eat meals in the mess compartment. On arrival, we spent time in the Brooklyn Navy Yard, getting some of that good New York liberty. Then in April we were part of the escort for a convoy of 48 merchant ships headed for Casablanca. We left from New York, and after the convoy was formed we began the zigzag course for North Africa. The speed of the convoy was eight knots. On the course we were taking, the Chief Quartermaster told me there were 82 reported sightings of submarines. This was our first real assignment that didn't have to do with just tests and drills. Oh, Captain Conley held many drills along the way. He was far from satisfied with our readiness for action. But our being with that convoy wasn't just play. There were troops in North Africa very much in need of the supplies we were shepherding. The trip took us eighteen days. Much to the relief of all, there were no submarine contacts.

Our problems were minor, mostly having to do with supplies running short. Eighteen days is a long time for a destroyer to be at sea without getting more supplies. Toward the end of the trip we were being served a great deal of chili and rice.

One of the bakers was planning on getting married when we returned to New York, so he was selling pies for a dollar each in order to increase his wedding fund. He didn't sell them to just anyone. He had to know and trust his customers. One night when we were standing the eight to twelve watch, Warren came into the chart house, and said with a great deal of excitement in his voice,

"I've got a pie lined up for us when we get off watch." That was grand news. We agreed to meet aft by Mount Four after we had been relieved. Since Mount Five was the ready gun we weren't likely to be seen by anyone. After I had been relieved I went back to Mount Four. IT was a beautiful night. The anticipation of the two of us having a whole pie to eat was like Christmas. I swear I could smell the pie before I could see Warren. It was still hot from the oven. As you can readily imagine, we had no utensils, using our fingers to scoop into our ready mouths. I don't know that I ever had tasted anything better. As you would imagine there wasn't much talk. When the pie was almost all gone Warren said,

"Hey, Souce, what kind of pie is this?" With deep appreciation and warmth in my voice I replied, "It's pineapple."

"Ack," he groaned, "I hate pineapple." It just goes to affirm that there are times in life when it is better not to know something.

As we approached harbor at Casablanca we received a message telling us to turn off our condensers because of the bodies still trapped in vessels that had been sunk during the invasion. Ten minutes after we entered the harbor the ship was covered with locusts. Ugly things! Someone said that the natives roasted and ate them. It isn't the kind of thing one would want to hear if seasick.

We were given liberty, half of ship's company for four hours one day, and the other half the next day. We were given instructions on how to relate to the natives, and where we weren't supposed to go in the native quarter. There were Military Police guarding each corner at the entrance to what was called "the Casbah" to prevent service personnel entering. Scuttlebutt had it that servicemen had gone into that section and disappeared.

A young lad attached himself to Browning and me as guide. We bought some pastry and offered him some, but he said he was fasting. Browning and I found a place filled with servicemen where champagne was two dollars a bottle. We were half smashed when it was time to return to the ship. Somewhere Browning had bought a piece of inner tube blown up like a balloon and tied to a stick by an enterprising native. As we passed along the street he would tap an Arab on the head with it. We had been told that they disliked familiarity, and that slapping them on the back was received like an insult. I could picture one of them pulling a long knife from inside his robe, and letting us know they didn't like getting hit on the head with Browning's balloon. When he did that I'd turn and salute the victim, and that appeared to mollify them. At least we didn't get knifed, or punched in the nose by a squad of angered Arabs. There were many of them, all male, just hanging around along the way back to the waterfront. Some of them had pictures they offered to sell. The pictures were of naked women. We looked, but didn't buy.

We were in port for only a few days. When we got underway again we escorted some merchant ships to the mouth of the Mediterranean Sea. Other ships met them, and we headed back to New York. I experienced no more sea-sickness other than feeling a bit queasy the first day out. As we entered New York Harbor the Captain had a commercial radio station piped into the Pilot House. Glen Gray and the Casa Lomas were playing, "*Don't Get Around Much Anymore.*" It reminded me of a girl back home. She had the Ink Spots' version of that song, and sometimes when we were sitting and talking that song was playing on her record player. Isn't it something how you can hear a familiar song, and in your mind you are immediately at a different place?

The Captain wanted to practice anti-submarine tactics. I don't know how such things were arranged, but just a couple of days after returning from Casa-blanca we went to the submarine base at New London, Connecticut. Each day we would go to sea with a submarine, and practice making depth charge runs. The submarine would submerge, and then we would try to find it on the Sound gear. When contact was made we would make a run, and simulate dropping depth charges. The Sub would release a smoke bomb when we indicated the first depth charges dropped, and that let us know how close we had come. The Cap-tain wanted the Soundmen to experience how the attack seemed from the other end, so one day I spent aboard the Submarine.

Each evening we would return to the harbor, and each night one-third of ship's company received Liberty in New London. I went ashore with Browning and Warren. We stopped in a bar for a glass of beer. A tattoo artist had his shop there, and was putting a tattoo on a sailor's thigh. With no intention of doing any such thing I said,

"I think I'll get tattooed." One of the others replied,

"Oh no you won't, we won't let you." For someone trying hard to be a man that was like waving a red flag to a bull. The first chance I had I ducked them, returned to the bar, and got an eagle tattoo on my forearm. For these many years it has been there as a kind of monument to the stupidity of this seventeen years old sailor. How can things like smoking tobacco, drinking alcoholic beverages, using profanity, and getting tattooed have anything to do with manliness?

Some weeks later while on watch a Storekeeper, whose last name was Grove, told me something about his Liberty in New London that I thought was hilarious. In order to communicate it to you I need to say that some ratings in the Navy were worn on the right sleeve. These were the ratings, which supposedly had come by way of the Deck Force, and carried with them an understanding of seamanship. The right arm rates were Boatswain, Gunner, Quartermaster, Signalman, Torpedoman, and Fire Conrolman. All other ratings were worn on the left sleeve. One of the requirements when taking the test for Third Class Petty Officer for one of the right arm ratings was to know *The General Prudential Rule* by heart. This had to do with the rules of navigation and was as follows:

> "In obeying and construing these rules due
> regard shall be had to all dangers of navigation
> and collision and any special circumstances
> which may render a departure from these rules
> to avoid immediate danger."

While on liberty in New London, Grove had met a woman, and they had shacked up. When morning came they didn't wake up in time, and Grove returned to the ship late. Consequently, he was on report and subject to appearing at Captain's MAST. As the day wore on he longed to get ashore again and meet his newly found friend. So about mid-morning he asked the Supply Officer, Mr. Welch, if there was any way that he could be allowed to go on Liberty? Mr. Welch replied,

"Gee, Grove I sure wish I could help, but you'll have to see the Exec about that" So Grove went up to Officer's Country, and knocked at Mr. McCornock's door. When inside, he told the Executive Officer what had happened, and that he was sorry about being late getting back to the ship. He also said that the scuttlebutt was that we'd be headed for the Pacific, soon and that there wouldn't be any good Liberty out there, and that he sure would like to see his friend again before we shipped out. He added that he knew he was technically on report, but he'd never been AOL before, and wouldn't be this time if the clerk at the hotel had called as he had been asked to do. Mr. McCornock said,

"I'll tell you what I'll do, Grove. You write *The General Prudential Rule* five hundred times and I'll let you have Liberty." Grove had a left arm rate. He didn't have any idea what *The General Prudential Rule* was, but the way Mr. McCornock said it he had the impression that he SHOULD know, and he didn't want to get in deeper by exposing his not knowing. Se he went out on deck thinking to find out, and write it five hundred times so that he could get ashore. As he got out to the main deck, Mr. Welch met him and asked,

"What did he do to you, Grove?" Grove said, "He told me if I wrote *The General Prudential Rule* five hundred times I could go on Liberty. What the heck is The *General Prudential Rule?*"

"Oh, said Mr. Welch, "that's the K.Y.P.I.Y.P rule."

"What the heck is that?" Grove asked? "Keep your peter in your pants," Mr. Welch said with a straight face. That made sense to Grove because he had been shacked-up, and it had caused him to be AOL, so he went to the Supply Shack and typed, "Keep your peter in your pants!" five hundred times. When he finished he brought it to the Executive Officer, and gave it to him. Mr. McCornock looked at it and said,

"Grove, what the hell is this?"

"Mr. Welch told me that's *The General Prudential Rule,*" Grove replied. Mr McCornock was not without a sense of humor. Grove was granted Liberty.

Our next assignment was on plane crash detail with the new Carrier, Princeton while she was on her shakedown cruise. For almost a month we operated with her out of Trinidad. That was soft duty! By this time there was no more seasickness for me, no more feeling woozy the first day out to sea. Each day we would be stationed on the starboard quarter of the Princeton about a mile or so back while she went through her tests. Some of the testing had to do with flight operations. There were times when a plane taking off didn't have enough speed to become airborne. It would hit the water, and quickly sink. It was our task to rescue the personnel. When a plane was forced to land in the water it was always a great relief to see the head of the pilot bob to the surface. It is no small feat of seamanship to bring 2,130 tons of ship close to a man in the water. Under wartime conditions there's no time to launch a boat to rescue someone. Captain Conley understood things about wind and tide and drift. He was a professional! He knew when to cut engines so that we could glide close to a man in the water without swamping him, throw him a line, and haul him aboard in short order. During the course of the war the Ringgold rescued fourteen airmen in just that way. Our days with the Princeton served well. It was time well spent.

Captain Conley conducted many drills during that period. At evening time we returned to port, and there was Liberty, one=third of ship's company allowed ashore at a time. The song, "Rum And Coca Cola" hadn't been written yet, but when it was it accurately portrayed a facet of Trinidad life for a sailor. "Both mother and daughter, working for the Yankee dollar." One didn't have to walk very far in Port Au Prince before a woman would hail, "Psst! Hey, sailor, you wan a good time cheap?"

When the shakedown period was over we left Trinidad headed for Norfolk. Something happened that was very good for me. As we headed north the wind kicked up. The Captain had given the Signalman on watch a message to send to a ship about seven miles away. So the Signalman, Ruvolo, was trying to send the message with the 36 inch search light because of the distance. It happened that the signal gang was short a couple of men, so he was trying to aim the light, and hold the message in his left hand, while trying to send with his right hand. The wind snatched the message from his grasp and blew it over the side. He had to go ask Captain Conley for the content of the message, telling him what had happened.

"How come your striker wasn't holding the message for you," the Captain asked?

"We're short of men," Ruvolo replied. "I don't have a striker." Captain Conley was not the most patient man in the world when it came to things having to do with one's job. But neither did he blame someone when they were doing the best they could. He gave Ruvolo another message, and told the Quartermaster to summon the Executive Officer to the bridge. When Mr. McCornock reported, the Captain said,

"Sam, the Signalman on watch just lost a message over the side because there aren't enough men on the signal bridge. I want that changed immediately!" The way I got word of this was Mr. Pembrook, the C Division officer, came down to C Division where I was in my bunk and said,

"Soucy, do you still want to be a Signalman?"

"Yes Sir," was my immediate response. "O.K." he replied, "you can begin standing signalman watches now." That's how I began the switch from Soundman to Signalman, from "ping girl" to "skivvy waver". It took me about three months to make Signalman 3/c, and I loved it. I was proud of being a Destroyer sailor, and I was proud of being a Signalman.

The scuttlebutt was correct, we were heading for the Pacific. We escorted the Princeton to Norfolk, staying there for several days to refuel and replenish supplies. Norfolk was commonly known by sailors as "Shit City". What that meant is that the Liberty wasn't very good. Norfolk had been a Navy town for many years, and undoubtedly not without cause, many of the people were not enamored of sailors. Since it was wartime, in most places servicemen were treated quite well, at least I was.

From Norfolk we went to New York, and that was a fine place to have Liberty. We were given a 48 hour Liberty while there, so I decided to go home. Joe Nave, who began striking for Signalman at the same time I began, came home with me.

It was to be my last time home for seventeen months, but I didn't know that then.

Not long after we returned to the ship we got underway again. As we left port the Captain announced that we were headed for Norfolk where we were to be joined by other ships, and then proceed to Pearl Harbor by way of the Panama Canal. On the way to Norfolk the Exec announced that when we arrived we were going to purchase a dog to be ship's mascot, and there would be a ship wide contest held to give the mascot a name. The sailor first submitting the name chosen would receive a prize of $50. There was no Liberty while in Norfolk, but Mr. McCornock went ashore and returned with a beautiful black Cocker Spaniel puppy. The panel of judges chose Sam as the winning name. He took to the ship as though he was at home. Maybe dogs don't get seasick. Sam sure didn't. We sailed from Norfolk with several other Destroyers forming a screen for new ships, among them two Essex class Carriers, and two light Carriers, one of them the Princeton. According to the scuttlebutt, the only large Carrier with the Pacific Fleet that wasn't damaged was the Enterprise. So we would be a welcome addition to Naval forces fighting the Japanese.

There was Liberty in Panama at Cristobal. I've not been able to figure out why, but there was something about the place that I found very depressing. The down feeling didn't last long, however. As a matter of truth I was looking forward to joining the Pacific Fleet. I knew very little about that part of the world, but I believed that the weather would be warm, and that was desirable for me, no more cold Atlantic winds. All Pea Coats were put in storage, along with cold weather gear. In addition, I had all my blue uniforms cleaned and stowed in my locker, anticipating that they would not be needed for a long while. The next port would be Honolulu, and whites the uniform of the day for Liberty.

The Pacific Ocean was impressive. The days were balmy, the sea calm. As the days went by I was becoming more adept as a Signalman. Night after night when we were in port I would flash a signal to a nearby ship asking if there was a striker who would be willing to practice. Receiving and sending messages by flashing light fascinated me. As my skill increased and Joe and I had responsibility for a watch section, my confidence grew. Something helpful along the way was that Chief Quartermaster White, who had been a Signalman, arranged the watch schedule so that he was usually on the bridge in the daytime when Joe and I had the watch. As I think back on it, White exercised a great deal of restraint. Either Joe or I would be receiving a message from another ship, and we would often get stuck on a word. White stood in the pilothouse keeping an eye on us, but he never interfered by telling us what the word was. We'd sweat it out while the sender on the other ship repeated the word as slowly as someone trying to communicate with a retarded child. In that way Joe and I learned visual communication.

I was on watch when the first island of Hawaii came into view. It was awesome for me. Until December 7,1941 I had never heard of Pearl Harbor. That day it exploded on the American consciousness. "Let's Remember Pearl Harbor" came from radios and jukeboxes for many months. Now we were preparing to enter that famous port. It was an impressive entrance. The Carriers led the way, the ships in single file. On each of the vessels, all ship's company not on Special Sea Detail were at quarters. The uniform of the day was whites for enlisted men, khakis for officers. On Ford Island we could see the damaged hanger. The Oklahoma and Arizona were still on the bottom of Battleship Row. I don't know how it was for the others, but I was awestruck. The brother of a classmate at Canton High School had died on the Nevada that day. He had left home a healthy young lad, and he returned as ashes in a container.

The Ringgold was assigned a place to moor alongside a dock. There was to be Liberty for my section the next day. It was an exciting time for me. I haven't said a whole lot about sex. That's intentional! Just let it be said, sex loomed large in my thinking. I'm the one who was afraid I would die before I got to try that. When I went ashore I had one aim. It didn't really make any difference to me how that came about. It made no difference whether it cost money or was free. Color of skin was not relevant. That the other person was female was just about the only condition upon which I placed importance. I felt that anyone who had the opportunity and didn't take it was some kind of fool. In any case, I don't wish to leave you with the wrong impression that every Liberty was some kind of lustful conquest or purchase. It didn't happen that way despite the fantasies of this seventeen year old. Honolulu, August 1943, the whole thing was treated like an appetite to be met. It was strictly a commercial operation. I recall some of the stores in Honolulu were open to the street. Several had a glass enclosed display case, and among the things displayed were snapshots of young women with bare breasts. I asked the male clerk, "Are there any whore houses around here?" He laughed and asked, "How high can you count?" It didn't take long to discover that there were many. Located in the middle of a downtown block would be a sign such as "Rainbow", or "Sunset", or "Roosevelt". There were stairs going up to the second floor, and usually up until ll:00 A.M. when they closed, a double line of sailors waiting to enter. Liberty was from 8 A.M. to 6 P.M. It was necessary to get in line for a bus back to Pearl Harbor before 5 P.M. if you wished to get back in time. We spent much of our Liberty time on the beach at Waikiki.

We would play ping pong in the Royal Hawaiian Hotel, which the Navy had taken over to be used by submarine sailors when back from patrol. Once I rented a surfboard that seemed to weigh almost as much as me. After dragging it into the water I paddled it way out, but I couldn't do anything with it. Finally I paddled it all the way back to the beach. Sometimes sitting on that beautiful beach I'd notice that a ship was headed out to sea, and the thought would go through my mind that soon we would have to go out again. That was a down kind of feeling. Often, we'd get underway and spend the day at gunnery practice, firing at a beach somewhere, or at a sled towed by a tug, or a sleeve towed by an airplane. One evening we got underway, and as we got beyond the nets guarding the entrance the Captain announced over the ship's speaker,

"This is not a drill! We are on the way to conduct air strikes against Marcus Island, 1,200 miles from Tokyo." Immediately after the Captain's announcement tension was high. Where sailors were gathered and talking there was a great deal of laughter. Although, I'm quite sure that had you asked any of us if we thought it was funny that we were on our way to attack Marcus Island the answer would have been "no."

The distance to Marcus from Pearl was no problem for the larger ships, but Destroyers don't have that kind of fuel capacity. On the way we rendezvoused with a support group that included a Fleet Tanker for refueling at sea. That's quite an operation. It's carried out while going about fifteen knots. The ships are joined by a line at the bow, the fuel hose comes across midships where the fuel trunk is located on a Destroyer. Aft on the quarterdeck a line is rigged for the transfer of supplies, or mail, or whatever. The ships maintain a distance from each other of about twenty yards. That's ticklish business. It requires good seamanship. The Captain of each ship has the conn of his vessel, and to facilitate immediate communication an Ensign with a sound powered headset stands by each Captain.

When we were alongside a larger vessel for supplies it was the Captain's custom to order ice cream for all of ship's company. Mr. Pembrook was the Ensign wearing the phones. Captain Conley told him to request fifteen gallons of ice cream. Mr. Pembrook relayed the message to his counterpart on the Tanker, and received in reply that they had already sent over ten gallons. Captain Conley told Mr. Pembrook to tell them we needed fifteen gallons. The word came back that they could only send us the ten gallons already sent. The Captain instructed Mr. Pembrook to pass the word to the quarterdeck to send back the ten gallons of ice cream. Mr. Pembrook said,

"Captain, don't you want o keep enough for the wardroom?" As long as memory works I'll not forget the Captain's response.

"Pembrook," he said, "if one man on this ship doesn't get ice cream, then nobody does."

As we completed fueling, and were preparing to return to the screen, an officer on the bridge of the Tanker shouted through a megaphone,

"Don't turn away too early. Make sure the bow line is free." Captain Conley still incensed by the ice cream shouted across through cupped hands, "Goddamit I'm not a Boot." A Four Striper on the Tanker said something to the Ensign wearing the phones, and Ensign Pembrook told Captain Conley that he was to put on the phones. The Four Striper talked, and Captain Conley listened. His eyes were flashing when he gave the phones back to Mr. Pembrook.

"I'll be dammed if I'll ever fuel from him again," he said. That struck me as funny since it implied that we had a choice regarding such things like the driver of an automobile choosing a gas station. All was not a bed of roses for the Captain of the ship.

The Carrier based air strikes on Marcus Island were scheduled to take place on my eighteenth birthday. I guess that I haven't mentioned that my battle station was on the bridge. I was one of Captain Conley's phone talkers. At the other end of my phones were Fire Control from where all gunnery was controlled, Torpedo Control, and Combat Information Center.

Drill after drill, practice and more practice had taken place in the previous months. I don't know how many times I had relayed the Captain's orders over that phone, and how many times I had informed the Captain of what had come over the phones from one of the three stations. There were times when the Captain was talking about things that I didn't understand. My brain was like a sponge, however, and after he had completed the message regarding the particular drill I was able to repeat it parrot fashion word for word. There were times, however, when the person at the other end would say, "Repeat that, please." Then I was in trouble, and I would try to repeat what I thought the captain was saying. It was from this that I got the idea that the Captain thought my second name was "Goddamit". He'd say,

"Soucy Goddamit, I'm the Captain! You say things over that phone the way that I say them!"

We went to Battle Stations at 3 A.M. The Carriers were preparing a pre-dawn launch. As I stood in the Pilot House I listened to the voice radio (TBS) between ships. Communications were kept to a minimum. Even though the distance of voice transmission was supposed to be about eight miles at the most, there was great reluctance to alert a listening enemy to the fact that a U.S. Task Force was operating in the area. Since it was still quite dark, however, all ships were darkened and no visual communications could be used except in extreme emergency. So, at night, any orders from the Task Force Commander were necessarily given over the voice radio.

Our presence only 1,200 miles from Tokyo was a complete surprise. The first wave of aircraft began their bombing and strafing runs before the sun was fully risen. The Captain secured a cook and some mess cooks from their battle stations to prepare soup and sandwiches for all hands. The sandwiches were passed out first. I had just prepared to take a huge bite out of mine when the message came over the TBS that a large group of about sixty bogies (unidentified aircraft) had been picked up by radar on one of the Carriers. I immediately lost my appetite, and handed my sandwich to one of the Signalman who happened to be standing there. The bogies finally turned out to be friendly planes returning to their Carriers, but it was too late to get my sandwich back. Some birthday meal!

It wasn't only the sandwich that I missed there at Battle Stations during the air strikes against Marcus Island. A short while after we were given the sandwich that I gave away when the bogies were reported, a mess cook brought a cup of soup. It was one of those thick Navy cups, and in the stress of the moment it never occurred to me that the soup had been ladled into the cup from a seaming hot kettle. The cup in my hand was cool. I took a big mouthful, and it was flaming hot. The Captain was standing close by, and I didn't dare spew it out all over the bridge. I sure couldn't swallow it, and for weeks after there was a blister hanging from the roof of my mouth. Ever since I've carefully checked the temperature before putting something in there.

After the raids on Marcus we returned to Pearl for replenishing supplies, and getting Liberty in Honolulu. It wasn't long, however, until we were on the way to conduct air strikes against enemy held islands of the Gilbert group. In the midst of the operation the Task Force had withdrawn for refueling. The Task Force Commander sent a message to all ships saying that it had come to his attention that the Task Force had crossed the Equator, and there were a large number of Polliwogs aboard the ships. (Polliwog is Navy for a sailor who has not been initiated into the ancient order of the deep after crossing the Equator.) The Task Force Commander enjoined the Shellbacks to get on with appropriate initiation ceremonies the next day.

I won't go into the details, but that was the worse beating I have ever taken in my life. Most of the crew, including the Captain and the Executive Officer, were not Shellbacks. It seemed to me that only about 50 sailors were doing the initiating. Joe Naive and I stayed on the Bridge for most of the day postponing it as long as we could. But we finally had to go through with it. For many days after that the sailors in the shower room were a sight to see with their butts a mass of yellowish purple bruises. During the initiation a fat colored officers' steward was the Royal Baby. He was dressed in a diaper, and had a ribbon tied around his head. The Polliwogs were made to crawl up to him and kiss his belly. I remember some of the fellows from the Southern States saying,

"I'll never kiss that nigger's belly!' After getting beaten with the salt water soaked thick line the Shellbacks were using I suspect they'd have kissed whatever in order to get away. So in the midst of war there was time for diversion.

During the air strikes on Marcus and the Gilberts no enemy planes or ships attacked the ships of the Task Force. Such was not the case on our next operation. We returned to Pearl Harbor, most of us with our rainbow colored bottoms. There was Liberty in Honolulu, and that provided a welcome change of pace.

By this time I was becoming a rather capable Signalman. Most of our work was with flashing light messages. There is a limit to the speed that a message can be sent because of the physical limitation of opening and closing the shutter on the light. Try to go to rapidly, and the dots and dashes run into each other, and the message is unintelligible. The sender transmits a word, and the receiver acknowledges reception with an answering flash from his light. If the receiver fails to give the answering flash, the sender repeats the word. My proficiency was such by this time that if the sender was good at what he did I could hold my light open and receive the message without any words being repeated. Most of the time I could do that. However, after we had been at sea for a while, and under tension, I discovered that I was not as sharp in receiving a message. Then after a stay in Pearl Harbor with several times of Liberty in Honolulu, I was rested and when we returned to sea I was again able to receive messages without stumbling over words. I was learning an important lesson. No matter what we do, we get stale after a time, and need a change of pace. Recreation is literally a kind of RE-creation, a necessary renewal if we're to function at our best.

I think that it was at this time that the Battleship Oklahoma was finally raised from the bottom of Battleship Row and put in dry dock. That left only the Arizona, of the ships that had been sunk on December 7, 1941, still on the bottom. There was something sobering about looking at the Oklahoma there in dry dock with the scars of battle so vividly evident. It was a reminder, if any of us needed it, that we were inv9olved in serious business.

Late September we got underway, and the Captain announced that we were on our way to conduct air strikes, and shore bombardment of Wake Island. The key words there for us were "shore bombardment". Also, that it was Wake Island made a difference. That small contingent of Marines holding out against the enemy in the early days of the war, and finally being annihilated was a sore spot in the consciousness of all our people. Wake Island had special meaning!

The journey to Wake was uneventful. October 5,1943 the Task Force began air strikes at dawn. A Task Group of Cruisers with a Destroyer escort was sent in to bombard shore installations. The Ringgold was part of the screen for the Cruiser Group.

As the Carrier planes began strafing and bombing runs we were on station, the Cruisers in single file, and the Destroyers patrolling ahead. We were about four miles from the island when the Cruisers opened fire. There were answering flashes from shore guns, and splashes began dotting the water in the vicinity of the ships. For whatever the reasons, the Destroyers were not supposed to fire unless directed to do so by the Task Group Commander.

Smoke from shore installations that had been hit by bombs, or shells from the Cruisers, began to rise from the island. Over the TBS there was an occasional report from one of the ships of a shell splash close aboard. The Fire Control Officer, Mr. Ensey, reported over my phone that he had enemy gun installations targeted, and requested permission to open fire. The Captain replied that he was trying to obtain permission from the Task Group Commander, and would give it as soon as received. Lieutenant Ensey said,

"Dammit, this is the way ships get sunk." And immediately added,

"Don't pass that on, Soucy." I was at a high level of excitement, but not afraid. In some strange way it all seemed almost unreal.

The planes from the Carriers had caught the enemy completely by surprise. Most of their planes were destroyed on the ground in the first attack. The Cruisers had launched their SOC-3 Float Planes for spotting purposes. One of them was attacked and shot down not far from where we were. A lone Zero had ducked out of a cloud and damaged the plane. I watched as two parachutes opened with their human cargo dangling below. The Zero made a strafing run on the airmen, but the ships were helpless. We couldn't fire at the Zero for fear of hitting our own men as they slowly sank to the sea. It was good to hear that both men had been rescued, and though one of them had been hit, they were both all right. None of that got into my feelings. It was about then that the Destroyers received permission to open fire.

"Tell Fire Control to commence firing." The Captain said. No sooner had I said the words than our five inch guns opened up. Instead of firing salvo fashion, all five guns firing at the same moment, each gun fired independently as soon as loaded. Pretty soon the paint on the barrels began to blister, and the canvas bloomers to smoke. Water was sprayed on the barrels to keep them cool. In a very short while all enemy fire ceased. I have no recollection of how long we stayed there. Before dark we rejoined the main force, and headed home to Pearl. We had received our baptism of fire.

Our stay at Pearl Harbor was longer this time. We had several opportunities for Liberty. There were days when we went to sea to practice gunnery, but there were days when we were in port and the routine was relaxed. The scuttlebutt had it that we were going to be in on an invasion. Toward the end of the month we got underway with other ships, and Browning told me we were going to the New Hebrides to practice for a landing in the Gilbert Islands.

By this time Sam was as much part of the crew as any of us. He spent a lot of his time on the Bridge. At morning Battle Stations the Captain often allowed Sam to lick the last bit of coffee from his cup. Whether or not men are meant to live on ships like that I don't know, but I'm fairly certain that such living is not meant for dogs. For one thing there's no Head as there is for the crew. When Sam wished to relieve himself he often chose my cleaning station on the port wing of the Bridge. Not always in good spirits I'd take up the mats, hose them off, and swab the deck. Most of the time we accepted that as part of the price of having Sam for a mascot.

Efate in the New Hebrides has a beautiful harbor. You enter from sea by winding up a channel between high hills on each side. It was like sailing up a river between those hills. I assume that there was a town of some kind, but we were never allowed ashore while there. There was a Naval installation, and an airfield. From the Bridge we could see an occasional civilian home through the long glass, but there wasn't much, and I don't think anyone minded not having Liberty. Each day we would go to sea with other ships, including Troop Transports, and rehearse an amphibious invasion. At evening we would return to Efate. Marine Corsair Fighter planes would meet us in the channel, weaving their way over us, not much more than masthead high. There was something awesome about the way they flew along that channel between the hills on both sides.

One evening Browning was going ashore on some errand and he took Sam with him. The installation was small, hardly any motor vehicles at work there. Sam was just like any sailor going ashore, he couldn't wait, and as the Ship's Boat got close to the dock he leapt ashore, and ran right in front of a Weapon's Carrier going by. He was not killed but he was in terrible shape when Browning brought him back. As the word got around, ship's company from the Captain down was shaken. The next day as we were on maneuvers the ship's Doctor decided he'd better operate on Sam because of internal injuries. Sam never wakened from the anesthetic. That evening, on the way up that channel into Efate, Sam was given a military funeral. The Corsairs flying overhead that evening were appropriate. We didn't replace Sam. I think there was general agreement that shipboard was no life for a dog. By the time we left Efate it was generally known that we were going to invade Tarawa. Browning had made First Class by then and he had access to documents that most of us didn't. I don't recall him ever being inaccurate in the word he would give me about where we were going. Surely enough, as we left that day the Captain passed the word that we were headed for the Gilbert Islands, and that we would be part of a group invading Tarawa.

When we were about half way there the Captain mustered the off watch crew in the mess hall, and told us about what was ahead. He said that the Ringgold and the Dashiell had an important part to play. After the Transports were on station off shore putting their landing craft into the water the two Destroyers preceded by two Mine Sweepers were to enter the Lagoon, fire at targets of opportunity until H-Hour, at which time we would bombard the landing beach ahead of the Marines. He said that we would be the closest ships to the beach, and in a good position to provide the Marines with covering fire. He told us of Army Bombers that would bomb Betio each day for a week before we arrived. He said that he understood that their Blockbuster Bombs would take the leaves off of a Coconut Palm for a distance of 100 yards. The Battleships, and Cruisers, and Destroyers, on the seaward side of the atoll were to begin shore bombardment at dawn. Carrier planes were to begin bombing and strafing runs at the same time. Then just prior to the landing Fighter Planes were to strafe. Captain Conley said that it was the Task Force Commander's hope to make this landing without losing a single Marine. It would be the first time such a thing had ever happened if we were successful.

As we got closer to the island, tension increased. There were sailors in their bunks reading their Bibles before lights out. That had no meaning for me, and I have to admit to feeling somewhat cynical about that, because when we were at a place like New York or Pearl Harbor I don't recall ever seeing any sailor with a Bible. However, I never mentioned that cynicism to anyone. Just as no one ever tried to tell me what I ought to do or think about God. I didn't doubt that there was God. It's just that whatever that was seemed irrelevant to my life. I wanted to do what I wanted to do when I wanted to do it, and the God I'd heard about didn't approve of some of the things I wanted to do.

The night before the landing was to take place the Task Group Commander sent the Ringgold ahead of the Task Group so that the ships could take radar bearings off of us as we steamed between the atolls of Tarawa and Maiana. So there we were, about eight miles ahead of the other ships well inside enemy waters. Around 2100 we were called to Battle Stations. Radar had picked up a surface target around seven miles distance. According to our orders no friendly ships were to be in the vicinity. The size of the pip on radar indicated a vessel about the size of a patrol boat.

The Captain notified the Task Force Commander by TBS, and he instructed us to make a torpedo run rather than fire with our five inch guns. Tarawa was not far over the horizon now, and the flash of our guns firing would surely alert them if they didn't already know we were coming. Mr. McCornock from Combat Information Center (CIC) reported that the target was moving in such a way that it was impossible to plot a torpedo attack. The Captain told him to keep trying as we closed on the target. In a very short time CIC said that they had a good plot, and the information was given to Torpedo Control. Directly, over my phones, came the word that two torpedoes had been fired. Almost immediately there came a cry from Fire Control that one of the torpedoes was running wild, and on a parallel closing course with the ship. The Captain immediately ordered hard right rudder, and we heeled to starboard as the ship swung away from the torpedo. I still don't know why the Captain didn't make a complete circle, but I imagine that he figured that the torpedo was well ahead as he gave the order to turn back to course. In a very short time there was a huge explosion, and Torpedo Control shouted on my phones that we had been hit amid ships. I reported that to the Captain, and he calmly replied that the ship would still be shaking if we'd suffered a hit. The torpedo had gone off in our wake. It must have been close aboard because the explosion jarred the ship far more than when we dropped depth charges.

In the meanwhile the Task Force Commander had sent the Cruiser, Santa Fe up to help us. He ordered us to open up with the five inch guns. Fire Control had been on the target all this time. As soon as the Captain told me to pass on the word, "Commence Firing" our guns opened up. The dark of night accentuates what one is feeling at such a time. The flash of the guns takes away what vision one has. We expended eleven salvoes and the target disappeared. The response of the Task Force Commander was, "Well done!"

When we secured from General Quarters I was too keyed up to try to sleep. I stayed on the signal bridge talking with the fellows on watch. From over the horizon a signal light began flashing in our direction. The Exec, who was on the bridge, called to us asking what they were saying. We couldn't read it. No doubt it was a challenge from Betio. I suspect there weren't many on the ship or the island doing a whole lot of sleeping.

We went to Battle Stations before dawn. The Transports were on station, and beginning to anchor. There was gunfire from shore batteries, and the Transport Commander requested permission to shift anchorage further out since shells were beginning to land close to them. The Task Force Commander gave the permission. Some of the ships had begun their bombardment, and as dawn broke planes from the Carrier Force were beginning their bombing and strafing. The Captain announced over the ship's speaker system that we were on the way into the lagoon.

Betio was on our starboard side, smoke and dust billowing up from the island. I don't know how many coconut palms had lost their leaves from previous bombing, but there were a whole lot of healthy looking trees standing. Just then I heard what sounded like the staccato rap of a 40 MM anti-aircraft gun close at hand. I looked ahead and either the Requisite or the Pursuit was surrounded by the splash of shells landing close to them. The staccato sound was their two 3 Inch Guns firing rapid fire at the shore batteries. It would have seemed funny had I not been frightened, for their shells were splashing in the water along the beach not quite reaching the land. Their Captain was urgently requesting on TBS that we help them. Captain Conley replied that Fire Control was targeting the shore batteries, and we would begin firing as soon as they were ready. No sooner said than done. The Captain had given the order for Fire Control to open fire when ready, and he had scarcely put down the microphone on the TBS when our guns began firing. As soon as that happened the shore gunners switched targets, and we were now the ones surrounded by splashes. During the bit of quiet between our salvoes, I could hear the flutter of shells passing overhead. The Captain told those of us in the pilothouse to squat down to make a smaller target for shrapnel. I was terrified!

The Dashiell and the Ringgold each had a New Zealand Naval Officer aboard who had been stationed on Tarawa before the Japanese take-over. Having first hand knowledge of the waters of the lagoon they were each acting as pilot to keep the ships from running aground. We needed 13 ½ feet of water and there were an abundance of reefs much closer to the surface than that. Captain Conley was moving the ship ahead on one engine until the pilot said that we were running into shallow water, whereupon the Captain would move the engine to reverse. His intention was to make it more difficult for the gunners on shore who were only 2,000 yards away. One of the other phone talkers reported that we had taken a hit amid ships. The shell had glanced off of #1 Torpedo Mount, and ricocheted down through the Sick Bay, and out the Emergency Radio Shack. It very fortunately had not exploded, and the Chief Gunners Mate had thrown it over the side. Ken Wells then reported that we had taken a hit below the water line, and were taking on water. The shell had hit the Board in the After Engine Room, also a dud, we now had only one engine.

I don't think I can adequately tell you the extent of my fear. It went through my mind that I was going to be killed in the next half hour. Hanging from the rail close to my head an officer had left his forty-five in its holster. I had the thought, "Why don't you take the gun and get it over with. You're going to be killed anyway." Just about then the Commodore who was leaning against the Engine Annunciator signaled for the starboard engine to go to two-thirds speed and he said, "Let's get the hell out of here, Tom!" The Captain quickly signaled the engine to stop and in an exasperated voice replied,

"What the hell you trying to do, Henry, run me aground?" I wouldn't want you to have the wrong impression. All of my desires were with the Commodore. I wanted to get out of there, but all of my respect is for the Captain. Our task was to provide close fire support for the Marines as they landed, and as far as the Captain was concerned we would carry out that task as long as the guns were above water.

Somewhere along in there the Captain began to use me to relay messages to the people at the other end of my phone. The fear didn't leave, but it became more manageable. Time had no meaning. I don't really know how long we were under heavy fire before the shore batteries were silenced. Landing Craft began bringing wounded Marines to us. The two Destroyers were the closest ships with a Doctor aboard. We were secured to Condition One Easy. That meant the guns were still manned, watertight integrity was maintained, but water was turned on, and food could be served. I watched from the Signal Bridge as landing boats came alongside with their cargoes of wounded. The ship's Doctor and the three Pharmacist Mates worked all that day and night trying to save those who were brought to them. We had twenty-eight walking wounded on board at one time as well as those more seriously hurt. Two of the Marines didn't make it, and were buried there in the waters of the lagoon.

Seventy-six hours of unimaginable violence. Enemy dead were 4,690. This included Korean workers. Only seventeen Japanese were taken prisoner. The

Marines lost 1,027 including Navy Hospital Corpsmen. They had 2,292 wounded, 88 missing and presumed dead. All of those men killed, or wounded, for possession of a small coral atoll. I remember many months later having to waken the Commodore in the middle of the night as we were preparing for another invasion. He said, echoing Sherman,

"War really is hell, isn't it Soucy!" These many years later, having had time to think I would say,

"Yes, it is hell, a form of insanity given legal sanction, and respectability, by governments."

The smell of the dead in the tropic heat is engraved upon my memory. So is the memory of a Higgins Boat bringing wounded alongside, its bilge pumps expelling blood rather than oily water. I recall the two dead Marines with a tarpaulin covering them lying in front of number one smoke stack, and I remember seventy-six hours of awful violence, people against people for a stretch of coral atoll on which none of them would have chosen to live.

After the island was secure, the Ringgold was sent to FunaFuti for temporary repairs. We didn't talk about it so I don't know how the others felt, but I had a wrung out feeling. It was as if I had added several years in a few days. From FunaFuti we went on patrol in the vicinity of Abemama. From there we returned to Hawaii.

In need of repairs, we were assigned to the navy yard. Scuttlebutt had it that we would be there for a while before the next operation. So there was Liberty, afternoons on the beach at Waikiki. The in-port routine was a welcome change. I missed Joe Naive. He had arranged a swap with a Sailor from the Millicoma, an oil Tanker, while we were at Efate. He sent a letter from the States saying that he had seen a Newsreel in which the invasion had been shown. I'm confident I answered. Our paths crossed again later on, but somehow we lost contact. I often wonder about shipmates like Joe, and I hope that life has been good to them. He and I did something together of which I'll always be proud.

At Waikiki there was a large outdoor swimming pool not far from the ocean. It was filled with salt water, and had a high platform of four levels with the top level forty-four feet from the water. One afternoon Joe and I climbed to the top with every intention of jumping off. There were children of ten or twelve years cannon balling into the water from up there, so I didn't see how we could climb back down the ladder. We were in no hurry, however, and we stood against the railing talking. A sailor climbed up, walked over to the edge and said,

"The heck with that!"

Go ahead", I joked, "what if you were on a Carrier and had to abandon ship?"

"If you're so brave," he scoffed, "let's see you do it!" So I walked immediately to the edge and jumped (before I could lose my nerve), and out of the corner of my eye I could see Joe's legs alongside all the way down. He jumped right after me.

Something took place during that stay at Pearl Harbor, which presents an insight into the kind of leader Captain Conley was. Admiral Bagley had taken over as Commander of the Hawaiian Sea Frontier. Things had gotten very regulation in Honolulu. Not only that, but all of the whorehouses had been closed. I suspect, without knowing for sure, that it had to do with the fact that women in the armed services were now being stationed in Hawaii. What would a clean-cut All American Girl have thought if she had seen the double line of sailors at each of those places waiting to get laid? Some on the ship said that with all of the service women now in Hawaii there was no longer a need for the whore houses, but that was just wishful thinking. Anytime I saw a service woman while on liberty she was invariably with an officer. Maybe some of the crew were able to date on liberty in Honolulu. I never heard of it if so. Of course there was a whole lot that I didn't hear about. In any case, regulations in Honolulu had really tightened up. If the Shore Patrol saw a sailor failing to salute an officer, or not wearing his hat squared, or even jay walking, the sailor was given a ticket, and required to return immediately to his ship or station. The next day a Guard Mail Petty Officer would bring to the ship the tickets that men of the crew had gotten on liberty. They were supposed to be on report, and subject to Captain's Mast. One day just as Captain Conley was at the Quarter Deck preparing to go ashore, the Guard Mail Petty Officer was handing a stack of tickets to the Officer Of The Deck. The Captain asked the officer what that was all about. He was told that they were tickets, which men of the crew had gotten while on liberty for things like failing to salute an officer. The Captain said,

"Give them to me." Then he turned to the Guard Mail Petty Officer and said to him,

"Son, the men on this ship don't even salute me, and I'm the Captain." Then he threw the tickets over the side.

I have sometimes wondered if the Captain ever got into trouble over something like that. Surely that Petty Officer told his superior what had happened. Well, I'll never know. I hope that he didn't get into trouble for caring for his men. He was a good Commanding Officer, and he had the respect of his crew. There were sailors who had to appear before him at Captain's Mast, and he wasn't easy on them, but apart from the kind of griping that is like breathing to the sailor, the men of the Ringgold that I knew were proud to sail under Captain Conley.

Late January we left Pearl with a Task Force to invade the Marshall Islands. Kwajalein and Roi were the specific targets. Our assignment was again to enter the lagoon and give close support for the landing. Many lessons were learned at Tarawa. Kwajalein was subjected to heavy Naval bombardment and Carrier based air strikes for forty-eight hours prior to D Day. The landing was set for February 1, and the day before, a diversionary bombardment of Wotje was conducted to throw the enemy off as to landing site. It was estimated that about three fourths of the Japanese defenders of Kwajalein were killed prior to the landing. 368 Americans were lost in the invasion. The lesson of Tarawa was well learned.

Eniwetok was next for the invasion forces. It was Kwajalein all over again. The Ringgold did not have a role to play. We were part of an escort for a flock of LSTs that arrived with supplies a couple of days after the troops had landed. There was still shelling taking place but we weren't in on that. Eniwetok Atoll was secure by February 27. More than 3,000 Japanese defenders had died. American casualties, dead and wounded were 716.

During the next months we were sent to the South Pacific to operate with the Seventh Fleet. At Buna, New Guinea I bumped into a soldier from Collinsville. Some soldiers stationed there had come out to the Ringgold, and they had been part of the Connecticut National Guard. I asked one of them if there was anyone from Collinsville, and he replied that Loren Heath was Sergeant in charge of a searchlight about eighteen miles out in the jungle. So I went ashore that afternoon, and went to the Communications Tent as he had suggested. The soldier on duty called by radio to where Loren was stationed. He told him that a sailor named Soucy was asking for him. Loren told him to keep me there, and he'd send in a truck. Surely enough in about an hour a truck arrived, and took me out to where Loren was in charge of a group of soldiers, which manned the huge searchlight.

Loren was surprised to see me. He thought it would be my older brother, Denis. He said,

"Man, the last time I saw you, you were in short pants throwing stones at a telephone pole." I was able to stay only a little while, since there was a deadline for liberty.

Loren had suggested that I try to get an overnight liberty so that we could talk more. I was late getting back to the ship, and the next day when I saw the Exec. Mr Ensey, (Mr. McCornock had been transferred to a command of his own) and asked him if I could have an overnight liberty to visit a friend from my hometown, he said,

"Soucy you were late getting back yesterday. You're supposed to be on report." I told him what had happened, and he said,

"Oh, go ahead. Who would believe someone being over leave in Buna?" Being a Plank Owner had its privileges!

It was a pleasure to visit with someone from Collinsville. Loren was eight or nine years older than me, but as we talked about people we knew the miles rolled away and home seemed closer. That was the last time I ever saw Loren.

In March, Destroyer Squadron 25, screening a Task Group made up of some of the old Battleships, which had been sunk at Pearl Harbor, took part in the bombardment of Kavieng, New Ireland. Return fire was heavy for just a short while. This action was diversion for landings being made in the Northern Bismark Archipelago. During April and May we operated along the New Guinea coast, taking part in the invasion of Hollandia. Noting the successful leap frogging of enemy strongholds in the Central Pacific, MacArthur began to do the same in the South Pacific.

In July we rejoined the Fifth Fleet, and took part in the invasion of Guam. The Commodore was Landing Craft Control Officer, and we provided close shore fire support for the landing. We were taken under fire several times, and one morning there were pieces of shrapnel about the decks. We had been at anchor when a lone Japanese Gunner tried to shell us in the middle of the night. When we went to Battle Stations I heard Captain Conley saying,

"I'll be lucky if I don't lose somebody tonight." Our luck held and no one was hit. While still at Guam, Captain Conley was relieved by Warren B. Christie, and given command of Destroyer Division 112. Ship's Company was mustered on the fo'csle for the ceremony, and it was not a happy occasion. Afterward I watched through the long glass from the Signal Bridge as the Captain departed in a Higgins boat with all of his gear. As the boat pulled away the Captain was looking back at the ship. My feelings were safely tucked away in cold storage, but he looked sad.

We rejoined the Seventh Fleet in August, taking part in the invasion of Morotai. The scuttlebutt had it that the Pilippines invasion was next. There was further scuttlebutt that the Squadron was going to go back to the States for overhaul soon. Mid October we headed for the Philippines. Browning told me that we were going to break off from the main Task Force, and land a small contingent of troops on each side of a channel between southern Leyte, and Panaon Island, to guard against enemy torpedo boats. He also said that the Squadron had received orders to go to San Francisco for overhaul as soon as the landing was secure.

For months sailors had spoken with awe of how difficult it would be to retake the Philippines. Now there was special gloom in the feeling we'd probably get sunk, and not get back to the States. However, our part in the landing turned out to be easy. There were no Japanese troops in the area where we were landing men to protect that channel. Natives had come out to the ships in their outrigger canoes, and when the landing craft headed for the beach, the men in the outriggers led them in. A single Japanese plane came over about dusk not much more than 2,000 feet overhead. All of the ships fired, but the plane was unscathed and finally left. The next morning we headed back to Hollandia. The word was officially passed that we would refuel at Hollandia, and then head for San Francisco. Excitement was high. It had been sixteen months, and we knew that there would be liberty and leave. Much of the talk was about having thirty days at home.

When we entered Hollandia the ship was scheduled to go alongside a Yard Oiler after one of the other ships of the Squadron. As we were waiting our turn I was using the long glass to scan the other Destroyers in the harbor. I spotted the Mahan on which I knew Dick Gorgen was stationed. Dick and I had been close friends all through the school years. So I went to the Exec and told him about my friend being over there, and asked him if there was any way that I could see Dick. In preparation for fueling, the Captain's Gig was in the water. Mr. Ensey said to have the Officer of the Deck call the Gig alongside, and to have the crew drop me off on the Mahan. I don't recall now how long he said for me to take, but I have to admit to a feeling of pride in having the Captain's Gig take me over to the Mahan.

Our visit was short, but it was good to see him. He said that his Squadron was relieving our Squadron, and that they were heading for the Philippines the next day. Apart from that we talked about the little things. Time and distance changes things, and even friends have a need to find each other again.

As soon as all the ships of the Squadron were fueled we got underway for Pearl. There was a general good feeling pervading shipboard routine. We were headed away from folks who wanted to kill us, and toward people who would be glad to see us. I told my mother in a letter that we were headed for the States, but I didn't say if or when I'd be home. I wanted to surprise them. I also wrote the girl with whom I'd been corresponding, and whom I thought of as "my girl back home". I didn't tell her either about when or if I'd be home.

There were sailors taking out dress blues, and seeing what shape they were in after sixteen months stowed in a locker. Down in the compartment there was a poker game going on much of the time. Paul Wagner and I had decided to do calisthenics each evening so that we would be in shape for liberty. Altogether it was a delightful time. Sailing under the Golden Gate into San Francisco Bay was awesome. It was November, and the weather was brisk. The uniform of the day was undress blues. The early morning sun was shining on the city, and I guess that I looked like a poor child with nose against the candy store window. The Exec was on the bridge and he said,

"O.K. Soucy, there it is! You can close your mouth now."

Our orders gave us forty-eight days alongside Pier 25. General Engineering and Dry Dock Co. was doing the overhaul. Half the crew was to be on leave at a time. Twenty-one days was allowed. If a sailor lived on the West Coast he had twenty-one days at home. If on the East Coast we received thirteen days leave and eight days travel time. The sailors who lived in other places had leave and travel time arranged accordingly.

After we were tied up at Pier 25 the Exec mustered ship's company, and gave us word on how to proceed with things like transportation. He also told us that if anyone had souvenirs no one would see us remove them from the ship, but after that we were on our own. I had a Japanese rifle that I had bought from a soldier in Hollandia. It was a gift for my little brother, Brian. I was in the section receiving the second leave. Those of us still on board had liberty every second day beginning at 1600. One of the signalman, was Mail Clerk, and he had the first leave so he asked me if I would cover for him, and it would mean I had liberty every night. That sounded great to me, liberty every night, I mean. I'm ashamed to say that I did a terrible job as Mail Clerk. One thing especially comes to mind. The first day that I went to the Post Office to get mail for the Ringgold I discovered that our mail had been piling up for weeks because of our heading back to the States. Parents and girl friends, not knowing we were on the way back, had mailed Christmas presents early. I didn't know about things like registered mail, and the need to have someone responsible sign off for it. I brought twenty bags of mail back to the ship. The only place to sort was on the fantail. There was no storage available to keep mail for those who had already gone on leave. Things like old newspapers and magazines I threw away, figuring that everyone would feel as I did. Being in the States, who needed or wanted out of date newspapers and magazines? I remember clearly a small registered package for one of the Ship Fitters who was on leave. I had no place to store it so I took it to the Machinist's Mate down in E Division who was Master At Arms of the compartment. I told him my problem and asked if there was someplace there in which the package could be safely kept. He said that he'd put it an empty locker, which would be locked until the fellows returned from leave. It never entered my mind that I should have him sign for the package. That Ship Fitter never received his package, and when his parents put a tracer on it, the sailor who had received the package from me said he didn't remember me giving him any package. That's part of the free floating sadness I have in me. That sailor's folks sent him a wristwatch for Christmas, and he never received it.

What can I say about that time in the States? Had I been able to write an order to a store to purchase the kind of liberty and leave time I dreamed of it couldn't have been better. Well, longer would have been better, but after months in which a few hours on a coral atoll was very occasional liberty, San Francisco was this sailor's idea of heaven.

There was a period back there when I had been trying to see how long I could go without touching dry land. Having four bottles of warm beer on an atoll was my idea of nothing to do. That beer always resulted in a headache. The scuttlebutt had it that the beer had formaldehyde in it to keep the bottles from blowing up in the tropic heat. Anyway, on the one-hundredth day of my personal contest I was assigned to shore patrol for one of those beer parties. I sill recall the sense of indignation I felt at my contest ending in that way. That kind of contest should be allowed the dignity of ending at a place such as San Francisco.

Sibon, Chief Yeoman, had been kind enough to alter my liberty card so that I was twenty-one instead of nineteen. Wagner and I had the "Downtown Café" on Ellis Street as our headquarters. There was a bartender named, Johnny Green, who befriended us. We'd leave the ship each afternoon. As we walked up Market Street, headlines on the newspapers would shout their reports of the battle of the Philippines, and ships tangling with the Japanese Fleet. This self-centered sailor didn't give a second's thought to any of that. All that I was caring about was "Good Old Me" and the fine time I was having.

The day finally arrived for catching the train home. It took four days, and the sense of anticipation mounted with each passing mile. I had made a deal with myself that when the bus got to the dip in the road where Dyer Avenue and Maple Avenue meet I'd let out a shout of joy. I did just that, and the other passengers knowingly smiled. As I got out in front of Joe Mac's Drug Store, my brother Denis was just walking up Main Hill. I hollered to him and he said,

"Boy, will Ma be glad to see you!" Since I hadn't written she thought I wasn't going to get home. Denis turned his car over to me for the time I was there. He even arranged to have a party in my honor over at the dance hall. After all expenses were met they gave me a gift of the rest of the money. It was a once in a lifetime kind of experience! Because of traveling by train I had to leave home two days before Christmas. That's one of the most difficult things I've ever done. Very early I had been taught that men don't cry, and learned the lesson well. It is a mistaken teaching. There are times when tears are the appropriate expression of the spirit's pain. I carried that sharp pain in my throat, and the sinking feeling in my stomach for many days. As a matter of fact I had mentioned the willingness to be over leave in order to be home for Christmas, but my mother said that she would worry too much. So back to the ship, and back to the war zone I went.

There's not a whole lot of value in telling you of my pain in leaving home. Neither is there value in passing it by as if it wasn't so. How can one reckon the source of hurt in any definite way? Leaving "the girl from back home" was certainly a large measure of that pain. The time we had together was golden. We said our farewell the night before I had to leave. Denis was at work when I left. My mother, and Pat, and Brian said good-bye at the house. No tears! We were well trained not to allow emotion to show. I walked down to catch the bus to Hartford, and waited for it across the road from Joe Mac's Drug Store. As I waited, Bill Gajinski came across the street and said,

"Are you going back already?" When I acknowledged that my leave was over, he said, "Gee, I wanted to give you a 'cartoon' of cigarettes to take back with you." Bill was an old fellow who lived in a shack up by Town Bridge. I have no idea where he got money to live on, but I'm fairly confident that he was just barely getting by. I received the intent as a gift, and it added to the lump in my throat.

The four days on the train going back were agony. I didn't know what to do with that pain so I did the only thing I could, I endured it. My mother had given me a book she liked, "*A Tree Grows In Brooklyn*", and I read it on the way back. It helped fill some of the lonely hours.

In spite of wartime travel conditions, the train kept on schedule, and I arrived back at the ship with hours to spare. The first week in January we got underway for San Diego where we held post repair trials. Everything found to be shipshape, we headed for Pearl Harbor, picking up the Battleship New York at Long Beach. Someone who had responsibility for disposition of ships must have been desperate. The New York was so old it would have been a kindness to sell it to the Gillette Company for razor blades. By January 1945 the shipyards of America had turned out many ships including Battleships. It was difficult to figure what good the New York would do, but not mine to reason why. The Senior Officer Present Afloat was aboard her, so the Destroyers took orders from him. As we headed out to sea he sent a message that was all gung ho about how we were going out to meet the enemy, and fight him with guns, and torpedoes, and courage. I half expected the Signalman sending the message to spell out "blood, sweat and tears" but at least the Admiral had the grace not to add that. It was bad enough as it was. He must have thought we were all a bunch of feather merchants on our first cruise. If Admirals fantasize he was probably picturing each Captain reading his inspiring message over the ship's loudspeakers to awe struck sailors.

When entering a significant Port it was customary for ship's company to be lined up at Quarters. Entering San Francisco the uniform had been undress blues. Until recent times Pearl Harbor had been considered the war zone. Since ship traffic in and out of port was almost constant, dungarees were the uniform of the day, at least on Destroyers. That wasn't good enough for the Admiral on the New York. Two days before arriving he sent out a message that undress whites was the uniform of the day. The sailors on the Ringgold couldn't believe it! I imagine all through Destroyer Squadron 25 it was the same. Red Quinn and I had the eight to twelve watch that night so we wore dungarees, figuring that no one would care. There were some messages, which Red had to take to the Wardroom for the Captain's signature. When the Captain saw him he asked him how come he was wearing dungarees. Red told him that since it was after dark the sailors going on watch had just put on dungarees. The Captain told him to tell the Officer of the Deck to relieve the men on watch one at a time so that they could go get into undress whites, the uniform of the day.

I couldn't believe it. I had been thinking of asking for a transfer to Submarine duty, and that settled it. Red was as indignant as I was, so I asked him to stop by the Yeoman's Shack and pick up a couple request chits on his way back from changing into whites. After we had both changed we filled out the request chits. I don't recall what Red put in his, but I said something about wanting to get into Submarines because I understood they were less regulation than other ships.

The truth is that I didn't really want to be a Submarine sailor. I'm not all that comfortable when I'm shut inside. I didn't even go in the Engine Room on the Ringgold, feeling that it was too far below the waterline. What I really wanted to do was be sent back to New London, Connecticut for Submarine School, because that was only a couple of hours from home. Before we got to Pearl, Lt. Ensey came up to me on watch and said,

"I understand you want to get into Sub duty, because it's less regulation than Destroyers". "Yes Sir," I replied in my best military fashion. He grinned and said that there was a time when if someone just looked at a Submarine going by they would find themselves transferred to Sub duty. He added that current practice was that if a sailor wanted Submarine duty they were supposed to be allowed the chance, so that if I was serious he would approve my request, and that when we got to Pearl I would be able to go over to the Submarine Base to see if I could quality. Suddenly, the "home town girl" didn't seem quite so far away.

It was a relief to sail into the Destroyer anchorage at Pearl. We were out from under the command of the New York, and the uniform of the day was once again dungarees. The first chance I had I went over to the Sub Base, and presented my approved transfer chit to the Chief on duty. He said that ordinarily, before a transfer was approved a sailor would have to undergo an underwater test in the water tower to show that he could handle the rescue breathing apparatus, but the next class wasn't until the following week. He went on to say that he knew that those of us on Destroyers were out of port most of the time so that if I was able to equalize air pressure on my ear drums in a simulated dive in a pressure tank I would be recommended for Submarine duty. I was told to report for the test the next day.

The Sub Base water tower in which drills were conducted was a prominent structure. I don't know how high it was, but it could be seen from anywhere in the Navy Yard or harbor. I felt fortunate that I didn't have to enter that thing at the bottom, and slowly go to the surface using some kind of breathing apparatus. Knowing myself I'm fairly sure I could not have handled that.

There was a group of about ten sailors that entered the pressure chamber the next day. After we were inside, the sailor in charge began to raise the pressure. I don't recall now how much pressure we were supposed to take in simulation of a Submarine submerging. Long before we arrived at that pressure there was a sharp pain in my left ear. We had been told that if that happened to yawn, or make a chewing motion. I did that but the pain just increased. When I told him, the sailor lowered the pressure for several moments, and then began to increase it again. The pain returned, and I had to be let out of the chamber. The memory is dim, but I think I was relieved that I didn't pass the test. The passing years have shown that I would not have made it as a submarine sailor.

When we put to sea we were part of Task Force 58 under Admiral Mitscher. Our destination was Japan. The Ringgold went almost to the mouth of Tokyo Bay as a radar picket while the Carrier planes bombed Tokyo. Several cities and Naval installations were bombed during the early part of the month. Then the Task Force moved to the area of Iwo Jima to provide air assistance to the Marines on shore. We then returned to the coast of Japan where Carrier planes continued to bomb targets in cities and Naval installations.

As you would readily guess, when the Task Force was not engaged in action against the enemy, there were many drills conducted for the purpose of maintaining combat readiness. One of those drills, on the way back to Ulithi for rest and replenishment, assumed the Japanese Fleet came out to attack Task Force 58. As part of the drill some of the Battle Ships, Cruisers, and Destroyers were to form Task Group 58.2, and proceed to intercept the enemy ships. We were part of that Task Group. Red Quinn and I had the mid-watch so it was a matter of disgust to us that we had to go to Battle Stations at 5 A.M. After getting off watch I fell into my bunk hoping that by some lucky break we wouldn't be called to Battle Stations. There was never enough sleep to be had. The sound of the General Alarm penetrated the cocoon of sleep in which I was wrapped. Feeling cranky, I made my way to the port side of the bridge, and planked myself down on the flag bag.

It was a beautiful night with a bright full moon. The sea and sky were touched with magic, but I wasn't feeling very appreciative. I was exhausted. Since we were at General Quarters it would not have been possible to sleep, but the other Signalmen well understood me lying on the flag bag after having the mid-watch. Signal traffic was such that we were putting in long days on the bridge as well as standing our regular watch. With Battle Stations thrown in every now and then the whole crew was worn out.

There was a great deal of activity in the Pilot House. Task Group 58.2 had been detached from the main force. As part of the drill another Destroyer Division had been earlier dispatched, and from a distance of about twenty miles they were to commence a simulated torpedo run on the Task Group. How it happened I have no idea. It was a bright moonlit night, the Destroyer Division was closing at a speed of 23 knots, about 45 degrees to starboard.

I had no interest in what was going on. It was all a game, and I was lying there feeling sorry for myself, and somewhat angry that a day out of Ulithi we were playing war games when what I needed was sleep. As if that wasn't aggravation enough someone began to test the collision siren, and it wouldn't blow. What it was doing was spewing hot water over the after part of the signal bridge, and that included me. So I grumbled a few choice grumbles directed at whoever was testing the siren. Suddenly the men who had been on the starboard wing of the bridge came running to the port side. Almost instantly the ship shuddered, and heeled to port. One of the Quartermasters, Joe Carson, had been sitting on the Aldis Lamp box with his back braced against the bulkhead. He was trying to stand up, but as the ship heeled the bulkhead kept him from rising. It was funny but obviously something was seriously wrong, and I didn't laugh. What I did was snatch my life preserver from the rail where it was hanging, and quickly put it on. By then the word was getting around. We had been hit by the lead Destroyer of the Division making the torpedo run. It had been the Captain trying to blow the collision siren. With the full moon the other ships had been visible for some time, and when it became obvious that a collision was imminent, the Captain was trying to alert the crew. We were struck just forward of mount one. The other ship had just begun to turn, and when she hit, her fantail came clear of the water, and she swung to port prying our bow off like one would uncap a bottle of beer. It is a good thing we were at Battle Stations with water tight integrity maintained. The O Division bulkhead kept the sea out of all compartments aft of there. As you can readily appreciate there was much confusion! It is amazing that other ships didn't collide. The ships dodging each other in pre-dawn darkness would have been something to see.

We were lying dead in the water. So was the Yarnall, the ship that had hit us. As it became lighter we could see our bow, still afloat up ahead of us. Gone was the paint locker, First Division compartment, both anchors, and much of the Chief's quarters. A Repair Party was shoring up the bulkhead in O Division so that we could get underway. The other ship had not been at Battle Stations, and they lost a man who was caught in the Chief's compartment. Their bow had broken at the keel, and was hanging on by the deck plates. They had radioed to Ulithi for a Sea Going Tug to tow them backwards so that they wouldn't lose their bow.

When temporary repairs were completed we were able to make four knots. Before leaving the area we sunk our bow with shells from the Forty MM guns so that it wouldn't be a hazard to navigation. We waited until the Tug Boat arrived, and took the Yarnall under tow. Together we limped back to Ulithi.

As you would guess, for the next several days there was a great deal of excited speculation about having to go to the States for repairs. Thinking about a long period in a Navy Yard with few watches, no Battle Stations, and the possibility of another leave brought joy to each of us. We went alongside a Tender, and their Ship Fitters immediately went to work building a false bow down to the waterline. While this was going on the Third Fleet was gathering in the lagoon for the invasion of Okinawa. It seemed strange that we wouldn't be going with them.

The Commodore sent a message to the other ships of the Division that since we were returning to the read area, and would be able to replenish men and equipment, if they needed parts or ratings we could spare they were welcome to them. Requests came in, and we supplied the other ships with many items. To my dismay the Sigsbee asked for a Radarman, and the Communications Officer said we could spare Paul Wagner. Can you imagine the kind of let down that was for Paul? To be thinking about liberty and the possibility of some Stateside duty, and then to receive word to pack his things for a transfer to the Sigsbee was a blow. Neither of us liked the Communications Officer. I don't know anybody in

C-Division who did. Paul felt that there was some vindictiveness in his being the one who had to go. He had been with the Ringgold since commissioning. There were other Radarmen with far less seniority than he had. We were in a Floating Dry Dock having the false bow completed below the waterline the day he left. I remember it well.

The Communications Officer was O.D. when Reveille was sounded that morning. He came down to C-Division and walked through the compartment telling the men to hit the deck. When he got to Wagner's bunk, Paul looked at him and said

"Bug off"(or something like that), and he added, "If you come near me I'll drop kick you across the compartment." Some of us thought that Paul should nave received a commendation. What he got was Captain's Mast and busted to third class before being transferred that day.

As the fleet got underway for Okinawa we were still in Dry Dock. In-Port routine was a breeze. After repairs were completed, we left Ulithi with Pearl Harbor our destination. There was still no official word about whether we would go to the States for a new bow. Hope was running high. It's the kind of hope that sustained us through many months. The Okinawa invasion was well underway when we departed Ulithi just before sunset. After the Special Sea Detail was secured, and the regular watch set I had gone to my bunk for some sleep since I had the mid-watch. As I lay there Hedge came off the 4-8 watch and told me that a very strange thing had happened. Over the TBS was heard a call for help from a Destroyer off of Okinawa that had been hit be a Kamikazi plane. It was trying to raise another Destroyer some distance from it. The TBS radio was designed to be useful for a distance of about eight miles. This was so that enemy ships or stations would not be able to pick up voice communications, the use of which were curtailed when close to where the enemy was known to be. The damaged ship was having trouble raising the other Destroyer because the distance between them was more than ten miles. What Hedge was telling me was that we were picking up the message more than 1,200 miles away. Not only that, he went on to say that the Captain had answered the calling ship, and asked if he would like for us to try and relay the message, and upon receiving an affirmative went on to do just that. I scoffed at Hedge. I told him that there was no way that we could relay a message between two ships ten or fifteen miles apart while we were 1,200 miles from them. He insisted that he had been present in the Pilot House when it happened. So I hopped out of my bunk, and we went and asked Johnson, a fellow from Maine who knew more about radio, and sound gear, and radar than anyone else on the ship. Much to my chagrin, after practically calling Hedge a liar,

Johnson told us about skip distances, and that what had happened was one of those strange things that happens. One of the many times that Ron Soucy has had to eat his words. Hedge was a good friend and gracious about it.

There was something delightful about sailing in the backwaters of the Pacific war zone. Sleep was much sounder for one thing. Prior to the Navy I was able to sleep deeply, but that changed. Now someone just had to say my name, and I was immediately awake. When the General Alarm sounded it lasted for 90 seconds. Sleep was undertaken with the expectation that the alarm would interrupt. When it did I was dressed, and on the bridge before it stopped. On our way to Pearl there was little danger, no more morning or evening battle stations, and sleep was great.

Upon arrival at Pearl we quickly learned there would be no State side duty for us. The details of the damage to us had been sent ahead, and a new bow was sitting in front of the dry dock waiting for us. It was disappointing, but only for a little while. We knew that we'd be in the Navy Yard for several weeks. No drills, far fewer watches, no one trying to sink us, and liberty.

There's nothing significant to tell of the time in the Navy Yard. Just that it was relaxing to be away from the war zone. When repairs were completed we escorted a new Carrier, the Bon Homme Richard, to Leyte Gulf to rejoin the Third Fleet (When Admiral Spruance was in charge it was the Fifth Fleet, when Admiral Halsey was in charge it was the Third Fleet) By late 1944 there were so many ships attacking the Japanese that they probably thought there were two different Task Forces.)

The armada assembled at Leyte was gigantic. When we got underway on July 1, it was for the purpose of attacking the Japanese mainland. The Fleet was so large that it was broken into three Task Groups, each of them with large and small Aircraft Carriers, Battleships, Light and Heavy Cruisers, and a Destroyer screen. The Groups were about ten miles apart, and a Destroyer was placed between in order to relay messages. The Mariana's Turkey Shoot had severely crippled the enemy's naval air arm, and the Battle of the Philippines left them with very little operating navy. So we sailed those waters unchallenged. Unchallenged by ships that is. The Combat Air Patrol saw to it that no planes got near the fleet. As we got close to the Japanese homeland, however, lookouts on the ships began to spot floating mines. In just that one day the Ringgold exploded four mines using 20 and 40 MM anti-aircraft guns. And we were just one ship. There were 105 American ships and 28 British ships present. BY that I don't mean to imply that all of the Destroyers in the screen sank or exploded mines, but there were a significant number that did. I didn't see how we could go through the night without some ships being damaged or sunk, But it didn't happen. How can one account for something like that?

Task Force 38 sailed at will up and down the coast of Japan. The last of the Japanese Navy was swarmed over by Carrier planes as they were found in port. By night, Destroyers and Cruisers conducted anti-shipping sweeps along the coast. We were part of such a sweep, steaming close to shore for 60 miles along Northern Honshu. One small fishing boat was found, and a Destroyer rammed it. By day Battleships, Cruisers, and Destroyers were shelling coastal cities. From the Marianas General LeMay's B-29's were turning Japan's largest cities into ash heaps. Sixty-six of their cities had been fire-bombed, and planes were dropping leaflets telling which cities would be bombed the next day. It is estimated that 300,000 Japanese civilians were cremated in those raids. Their industry was at a stand still. Submarines had effectively blockaded inter-island shipping. Pearl Harbor had been avenged many times over. On the night of July 30, as part of Destroyer Squadron 25 we were ordered to enter Saruga Wan, a bay south of Tokyo. Our mission was to go inside the harbor for a distance of 35 miles, sink any ships encountered, and bombard the city of Shimizu at midnight. Shimizu, an industrial city of 60,000 lies at the foot of Mt. Fujiyama and photographers were with the Squadron to try and get pictures for the folks back home. Admiral Halsey sent a message of encouragement to the Squadron which included instructions should a ship be damaged to the extent that it couldn't be taken under tow in half an hour, the crew was to be transferred and the ship sunk. That didn't do a thing for my anxiety about the venture. Maybe, just maybe, under ideal conditions in broad daylight it may be possible to get a Destroyer under tow in half an hour. I'm very skeptical about that. At midnight in enemy waters with who knows what kind of interference it couldn't happen. I could picture hitting a mine, and having to swim to shore. When we talked about falling into the hands of the enemy it was always in terms of being tortured, so the thought of having to swim ashore on the main island of Japan was not a pleasant thought. We separated from the Task Group at 1645 to carry out our mission. The Captain announced that the Task Force would close to within 75 miles in order to provide us with air coverage. Two night-flying Corsairs would be overhead. There was no sleep that night, all hands to Battle Stations at 2142. The entrance to Saruga Wan is many miles wide. We entered close to the north shore. From the ship it looked as though one could almost reach out and touch the land. We were steaming at 30 knots. I had never seen water so phosphorescent. To me it was as if the ships were in the glare of a searchlight. I kept waiting for shore batteries to open fire. It never happened! No ships encountered. No planes in the air except our two. It was as if a squadron of enemy Destroyers entered San Francisco Bay and bombarded that city, and no one able to do anything in retaliation. At midnight we began our bombardment of Shimizu. Although we fired for only three minutes seven Destroyers can expend many rounds in that amount of time. When the order came to cease firing, the ships headed for the open sea at a high rate of speed. It was a relief finally to pass the harbor entrance. We had been inside for four hours. The light from fires burning back at Shimizu could be seen for a distance of 20 miles. Japan was a badly beaten enemy. Not because of this little thing we had done, but what we had done on top of all the rest should have made abundantly clear to even the most die-hard militarist that there was no hope. To prolong the war meant only hardship, suffering and death.

The Ringgold had a kind of newspaper. It was nothing fancy, consisting of two mimeographed pages of news items copied by the Radiomen on watch at night. Usually there was an item about current activities in which we were involved. These would contain a kind of box score in which enemy planes destroyed in the air or on the ground would be listed. Then at the end it would say something like, "U.S. losses were light, eight aircraft were lost, and only five pilots." I can recall thinking that to those five pilots our losses didn't seem so light. Task Force 38 was still conducting raids upon Japan when the ship's newspaper carried the news of the atom bomb dropped on Hiroshima. Even the early estimates of destruction caused by that one bomb read like something out of Buck Rogers. My mind couldn't comprehend such a thing. I had two thoughts at the time. The first was a question in my mind that if they had such a thing, why did they risk seven Destroyers and their crews just a week before, inside Saruga Wan? The second was the hope that the story of the bomb was true, and that the war would cease so I could go home. It was the topic of conversation in the mess hall at breakfast that morning. Mainly there were expressions of awe that one bomb could work the kind of havoc described in that news item. Also, there were the many expressions echoing my own feelings that this would get the war over more quickly and we'd be able to go home. There was just one dissenting voice. A Gunners Mate, whose name was Stan Gierlach said,

"We never should have dropped such a thing." I thought he was crazy, but that was when life was centered in good old me.

Japan was defeated before the bomb was dropped, but as Richard Frank so graphically establishes in his book, "*Downfall*" those in power had no intention of surrendering unconditionally. It is very difficult to end a war. One of the reasons it is difficult is because of how some in charge think. There are some people who seem to find a special kind of fulfillment during a war. This is an example of what I mean. One evening after darken ship the striker had taken the latest messages from the Signal Bridge and the Radio Shack to be signed by the Captain and ComDesDiv 50. One of the radio messages told of an indication that a representative of the Japanese government had put out peace feelers through the Swiss. Word of this quickly made the rounds, and it was most certainly a delightful thing to hear. However, when the Commodore saw it he said,

"This war can't be over yet, I've got more anti-shipping sweeps to make!" That's what I mean about a certain way of thinking.

When we rejoined the fleet, Admiral Halsey sent the following message to the Squadron Commander:

> "Loud applause to you and your boys for a well
> planned sweep conducted in the best Destroyer
> tradition X You have been enrolled on the
> Emperor's black list X Halsey"

The Commodore sent a message in reply suggesting that DesDiv 50 be sent into "Sagami Nada Rat's Nest to pick up the emperor's white horse and return it to the Admiral." When I sent that message I was thinking that the Commodore sure hadn't asked me if that's what I wanted to do. What I wanted was to stay alive.

August 15, 1945 is etched upon my brain like acid etches steel. I had the 4-8 watch. As it got light the Carriers launched planes to conduct strikes against Tokyo. After I was relieved I had breakfast, and took a shower in anticipation of a bit of rack time. I'd just gotten into my bunk when the Commodore announced to all hands that we had received word to cease all offensive action against the Japanese Empire. The war was over!!

The Third Fleet remained off the coast of Japan. The afternoon of the fifteenth Admiral Halsey spoke to the men of the Task Force over TBS. He began by saying that we were now in a peaceful relationship with the Japanese. Then he added it was possible that there would be fanatical people in the military who would want to continue hostilities, and that we must remain alert in case Kamikazi pilots came looking for our ships. He said he had instructed the Combat Air Patrol to be vigilant, and if they met any Japanese planes they were to shoot them down in a friendly fashion. I don't remember anything else about the Admiral's speech, but I wish I had a tape of it. Admiral Halsey had the respect of this sailor, and I never heard a disparaging word regarding him.

For several days it was very unclear about how Japan would be occupied. One of the early plans was to use the sea going Marines from the larger ships with a supplemental force made up of sailors from each ship. I don't recall now for sure, but I think that each ship was instructed to pick ten percent of the crew with experience in things like rail-roading, medicine, communications, etc. I was in the group on the Ringgold, because I was a signalman. When the occupation forces weren't taken from the Fleet, it was a disappointment for me.

We weren't in Tokyo Bay for the peace signing. One of the Carriers needed an escort to Guam, and we were assigned that task. When we arrived at Guam we were given orders to proceed to Saipan to pick up passengers, and then go to Newport, R.I. by way of the Panama Canal with stops at Pearl Harbor and New York City. What an exciting time! At Saipan we received about 25 passengers. When we got underway there was no more "darken ship" at sunset. The ships were lit up. We could communicate with each other at night using flashing light. The wartime song of hope, "When The Lights Go On Again, All Over The World" was being realized before my eyes.

What an awesome experience that was. Something not quite so awesome was a restriction that was posted two days after the war ended. Enlisted men were no longer allowed to smoke in the Pilot House. Not only that, all bright work that had been painted during the war was to be scraped and shined. Had I needed confirmation that a career in the peacetime Navy was not for me, that would have done it.

When we arrived at Pearl, as soon as I could get over to the Navy Yard I went looking for the Sigsbee. She was in Dry Dock, and as I walked along the pier Paul Wagner saw me and came running down the gangway to meet me. We had a good visit. Being several years older than me, and having his mother as a dependent he had enough points to be discharged in September. When he learned the Ringgold was going to be in Newport for Navy Day he said that he would take my mother there for the celebration. What a good friend. It was a joy looking forward to that.

Panama was as bad as I remembered it. As the ship entered the canal, and the Pacific Ocean receded into the background, I looked aft and said "Good Bye, Pacific Ocean this is the last time you'll ever see me." Hedge and I went ashore together. We sat in a bar drinking Panamanian Beer. There hadn't been a whole lot of beer drinking in the past months, and the local beer had a higher alcohol content. In three years it is the one time that the Shore Patrol picked me up. We were brought back to the ship for our own safety.

Out of a crew of 323 there were about 55 of us of the original crew, which had put the ship in commission. Many of those now on board had never sailed in the Atlantic Ocean. No matter how rough the seas during those months in the

Pacific those of us who had been in the Atlantic used to tell the others that they hadn't seen rough water until they sailed Cape Hatteras. Wouldn't you know it, when we went past Cape Hatteras the ocean was like a mill-pond?

When we sailed into New York harbor it was a heart grabbing experience. Twenty-six months had gone by since I had my last glimpse of the Statue of Liberty fading into the distance astern. Now there she was again in all her glory. Over on the shore in large while letters there was spelled out the words that raised a lump in the throat of many returning servicemen.

WELCOME HOME
WELL DONE

Liberty in New York, and then in New London was just marking time. The big thing looming large was getting discharged. At my age and with no dependents had I joined the Navy on the day Pearl Harbor was attacked, and spent the whole war on sea duty I still would not have enough points to get out. It looked as though it would be into the new-year before that event.

Hedge and I went on liberty in New London, sat in a bar drinking beer listening to Harry James and the band playing, *"It's Been a Long, Long Time"*. He called his girl, and introduced me to her over the telephone. I tried to call the "girl back home" but wasn't able to reach her.

When I returned to the ship we had our orders to report to the Navy Yard at Charleston, South Carolina to put the Ringgold in mothballs for de-commissioning. All of ship's company, not eligible for discharge in the next six months, were granted 30 days leave. That let me out. I'd been in the Navy for thee years and two months. In that period I had a total of twenty days leave. Fellows who had been in the Navy for less than a year, and on board the Ringgold for three or four months, were receiving more leave at one time than I had received the whole time I'd been in the Navy. I felt hard done by. However, one consolation was that the requirements for discharge had been liberalized and I was eligible December 1st. Liberty in Charleston was of no interest. I worked on the Signal Bridge days, went over to the PX occasionally and drank beer, took the duty as Gangway P.O. for others so that they could go on liberty, and waited. Lt. Flynn was acting Exec He was the only officer left who had been in ship's company when the Ringgold was commissioned. He was a good officer. Something got fouled up so that those of us who were to leave the ship December 1st weren't able to go. It never was clear to me just what happened. Lt. Flynn apologized to us and said that we had a free gangway, which meant we could come and go as we pleased. I kept the same routine. Liberty in Charleston was my idea of nothing to do.

Finally on December 9, we left the Ringgold for the last time. Several of us had orders to report to Lido Beach Receiving Ship, Long Island, N.Y. to be processed for separation. We spent three days at Lido Beach. It was pretty relaxed. There were seminars about returning to civilian life. One officer had the task of encouraging reenlistments. He apologized to us when he began his talk. There were no takers from our group. We had a complete physical, of course. Mike Annis, one of the sailors from the Ringgold, suggested that it was wise to complain of backaches because if one had back trouble later on the government would be responsible for care. I admired his courage in doing that. Even if my back had hurt I would have kept it to myself. I didn't care to take a chance on the discharge being delayed for any reason.

Finally the big day arrived! We each received what pay we had on the books, plus $300 mustering out pay. In addition we were compensated for leave not received on a basis of thirty days annually. So I received an extra 77 days pay. I felt rich, and proud of the ruptured duck sewed to my uniform as sign that I was honorably discharged.

3

After The War

Red Quinn lived in Hartford, so of course we caught the train at Grand Central together. A pan-handler put the touch on us, and we gladly gave him a dollar each. Immediately two men grabbed him, and made him give it back. I guess they were railroad people. They said that he watched for discharged servicemen because he knew that we were all feeling good about being discharged, and that we had our mustering out pay. Red invited me to stay overnight at his house so that we could go shopping for civilian clothes that afternoon. We did that. I bought three sports outfits. For three years, three months and ten days I hadn't worn civilian clothes. I wore my uniform home the next day because I was proud of having been a sailor. My mother was glad to see me. That evening I dressed in one of my new sport suits, and when I came downstairs my mother said,

"Oh, I was hoping you'd wear your uniform for a while, you look so good in it." I thought that I looked pretty fine in civilian clothes. I was proud of being a sailor, but there was no way that I intended to put that uniform on again.

Getting discharged from the Navy was a very important moment in my life. I've often wished that at the time I had gotten off somewhere by myself. I had an unrecognized need to sit quietly, and allow the wonder of it all to wash over my being. In those years I had the feeling that if life didn't seem too good something would happen to make it better later on. I don't know what I thought being a civilian would be like, but in anticipation I had been as sure as could be that life would be great. It didn't happen that way. I had no idea what I was going to do. When I'd been asked that question during the separation process I had said that I wanted to go back to school. Hedge and I had fantasized about going to the University of Syracuse, School of Journalism, but I only had one year of high school. During the last months on the Ringgold I had taken GED tests, and shortly after arriving home I received a Connecticut State High School Diploma. However, I didn't think there was any way that I could enter college.

New England winter seemed awfully cold after two years in the Pacific. I stayed around the house

Listening to Martin Block's, "Make Believe Ballroom" in the afternoons, and went down to Leo's at night. I needed that period of just doing nothing.

I hadn't done any serious thinking about what I would do after discharge. Now I know that I was very much in need of counseling, but I didn't know it then. I just assumed that eventually I'd get a job and get on with life. With my one year of high school I wasn't qualified for anything that seemed appealing.

The 'girl back home' wasn't around. The truth of the matter is that although we had corresponded regularly, and had spent a great deal of time together during that leave, she wasn't really my girl. I began dating a girl who lived down the street. She was a senior in high school, and exactly what people in those days meant when they spoke of a 'nice' girl.

My days had not very much direction. I'd spend time at Leo's shooting pool, just hanging around. After supper I'd take Dorothy to a movie. My mother was working at an insurance company in Hartford. It must have concerned her that I wasn't aiming for something. She had long had the hope that I would go to college, but she didn't crowd me. Finally in late spring I got a job at an Army convalescent hospital for blinded veterans as a chauffeur-mechanic.

Old Farms Convalescent Hospital had been a private school for boys before the war. The Army had taken it over for the purpose of teaching veterans who had lost their sight how to be self-sufficient. So my job in the motor pool had a civil service classification. For 95 cents an hour I drove Army vehicles, most of the time transporting a group of veterans somewhere. It was a good job. I enjoyed it, but something was not right. At times I felt frightened without knowing why. Often the muscles in the back of my neck felt tight. One evening at the movies there was a strange feeling in my right hand, a tremor like quiver that lasted a few seconds. It never occurred to me to mention this to anyone. I dealt with it by trying to ignore it.

Dick Gorgen's mother and father ran the theater, and one evening they told me that Dick and his wife were coming back to Collinsville. That was good news! After his ship was sunk Dick had gotten shore duty at Port Chicago Naval Magazine. While serving there he married a young woman from a nearby town, and they had a child. I was eager to see Dick and meet his wife and daughter.

Dorothy and I had been dating since January. We talked about getting married. It seemed like the thing to do. I had the distinct impression that her father didn't take to me, but I asked him if Dorothy and I could get engaged and he gave his permission. I thought I was doing what a fellow is supposed to do. I had a job, was engaged to get married to a nice girl, but something was wrong.

Dick and his family arrived in July. They stayed with his folks, and Dick went to work for New Departure Division of General Motors. Dorothy and I double dated with Dick and his wife, Nadine. One Sunday we had gone to church with them. Church had no meaning for me. It certainly wasn't part of Dorothy's life, and I'm pretty confident that it wasn't Dick's idea of what to do on a Sunday morning. However, I gathered from things he said that it was important to Nadine. On the way home afterwards Dick said,

"I can't stand it here, Souce! We're going back to California on Wednesday." In an off-handed way I replied,

"I wish I was going with you."

"Come along," Dick said, "we'll split the driving." This was a totally new idea to me. The thought of leaving Collinsville had never entered my mind. I looked at Dorothy and said,

"I could go out there and get a job and send for you." She responded in a positive way. That's all it took. When I got home I said to my mother,

"I'm going to California on Wednesday with Dick and his wife."

"It's this damn war that made you like that," she replied. I didn't feel that the war had a thing to do with it, but it wasn't worth arguing about.

Work with blinded veterans was winding down at the convalescent hospital. There were constant rumors of cutting back. So, my terminating on short notice wasn't frowned upon. I said good-bye to Dorothy Tuesday night. She cried a little, but the thought of us getting married, and living in California was exciting for her and we parted on that note. Leaving was not difficult for me. I was looking forward to new places. It wouldn't have made any difference to me if we were headed for Texas or Alaska. I wasn't happy where I was, and I thought that being someplace else would solve that.

It was just beginning to get light when Dick stopped by for me on Wednesday morning. My mother was still in bed. I said good-bye, but if she answered I didn't hear her. Dick's car was a 1941 Ford Coupe. There was plenty of room for thee adults, and they had a little bed fixed up for Diana on the shelf in the back of the seat. Dick and I did the driving. When it was time for Diana to eat we would stop and insert a piece of cardboard in front of the radiator. After the water temperature got close to boiling we'd stop and drain some of the water into a coffee can, and warm Diana's bottle that way. For our meals I'd stay in the car with Diana while Dick and Nadine ate, and they would stay with her while I ate. When we stopped driving for a day we'd get a motel room with two beds. They slept in one, and I had the other. We split expenses three ways. It was an exciting time.

The Ringgold had covered more than two hundred thousand miles. I'd been to places like Casa Blanca, Cuba, Trinidad, Panama, Hawaii, Guam, the Philippines, and a large number of atolls. Now I was seeing my own country. We took the Pennsylvania Turnpike, which was fairly new then. I hadn't dreamed that there was a highway such as that. After leaving the Turnpike we angled southwest and picked up Route 66 north of St. Louis.

Each day presented me with new things and places to see. "*Get Your Kicks on Route 66"* had been popular that summer. Sung by the Andrews Sisters, or Nat Cole, the song had been part of the background music while shooting pool at Leo's, or getting a milkshake at Christie's after a movie. Now the places of the song were a reality: St. Lous, Joplin, Oklahoma City, Amarillo, Flagstaff, Winona, Kingman, and Barstow. We left 66 at Barstow and went northwest to Bakersfield, and then up 99 to where Nadine's folks lived outside of Pittsburg, about 30 miles from San Francisco.

I was impressed with California. It was warm! There were Palm Trees! The people seemed different than people back home. I can't put my finger on how they seemed different. They just seemed different. We stayed with Nadine's parents until we found employment. They were very gracious to us. It must've been difficult enough to have daughter and son-in-law and grandchild move in, but to have a total stranger too, must have been quite much. They were Nazarenes, which I gathered was a strict group of people. Nadine had been raised that way, no make up, no dancing, no movies, that sort of thing. However, they did not put a great deal of pressure upon us. We attended services on Sunday. And one Friday evening they leaned upon us a little to go to a young people's meeting. Dick and I supported each other's feeling that it wasn't the sort of things we cared about, but were in agreement that it was a small price to pay for their hospitality.

We soon found work at Port Chicago Naval Magazine as Firemen. A large number of small ships that had been decommissioned were moored there, and there was a Ship Maintenance Department, which had the task of caring for the vessels. Two Fireboats were assigned to the department, and Dick became a member of one crew, and I was part of the other crew. We would be on shift for 24 hours, and off for 24. Most of the men working in Ship Maintenance stood watch on the nests of ships. There were occasions when someone from the Fireboat crews had to sleep on one of the moored vessels. It was dark and cold and clammy, not great duty! Now and then when short of watch standers we would have to take an eight-hour watch on one of the nests of ships. In some ways it wasn't unlike being back in the navy.

Dorothy and I had been corresponding regularly, of course. Some of her letters left me with negative feelings. The thought of getting married was still there, but getting married in my thinking represented steady sex rather than being so enamored of another that I could not imagine living without them. I had no idea of what loving another person was.

Dorothy had talked with her parents about coming to California. Her father told her there was no way that he would allow her to go to California not married. He said that if I wanted to marry her I would have to come back to Collinsville. That seemed like a lot of added expense for a young couple just starting out, but I could understand his reluctance to have her come to California, and then something go wrong with the relationship. So I made arrangements to have the time off work, and we drove to San Francisco so that I could make reservations to fly back to Collinsville.

The first time we drove into San Francisco I was amazed by the traffic on the Tunnel Strip into Oakland, and then across the Bay Bridge. I'd never seen anything like that, but Dick and Nadine were as casual about it as if they were on a Sunday drive along a country road. While in the city I walked up to Powell Street and along Ellis to see if places I'd known when on liberty in 1944 were still there. To my surprise Bunny's Waffle Shop, and the Downtown Café were no longer there. That kind of discovery always disappoints me. There's something in me, which believes that things ought to remain the way I experience and remember them.

A couple of weeks before my scheduled trip to Collinsville it dawned upon me that it would be a great mistake for me to go back there and marry Dorothy. If that thought had been in the back of my mind I wasn't aware of it. However, one of Dorothy's letters brought that home to me so clearly that I felt panic. I told Dick and Nadine that I wasn't going back. They expressed surprise, but I think that all along Dick thought that getting married wasn't the greatest move in the world. Writing Dorothy wasn't an easy thing to do, but I knew I had to do it. I'm fairly sure that receiving that letter was painful for her. I'm sorry for the pain I've inflicted upon others, but my not marrying her was without doubt the greatest favor I ever did for Dorothy.

More and more I disliked standing watch on a nest of ships when someone didn't show up for work. In January Dick and I were sent to Treasure Island for a week of training in fighting ship fires. I had the feeling that after the training they would no longer use us as watch standers. However, the first day back after our training was completed my name was called out to go on watch. I told the watch captain that I wasn't going to do that, and that I was through with that job. Dick immediately said,

"If He quits, I quit too!" It amazed me that he would do that with a wife and baby, and when I told him that on the way out he replied,

"Ah a good man can always get a job." So that was the end of our careers as firemen.

Several of Dick's friends had been stationed with him at Port Chicago during the war. They too had married local girls and remained in the area when peace came. One of them, Phil Arezzi, wasn't married, but he had stayed in that part of California, and worked for Associated Oil at their Avon Refinery. He liked his job very much and encouraged Dick and I to apply for work there.

We were both hired, so we were out of work less than a week.

It was necessary to begin in the Labor Gang. Openings through out the Refinery were posted on the bulletin boards, and one could bid on the job. When enough seniority was acquired you could then move up the ladder to a more desirable position. I do not recall now how long we remained in the Labor Gang, but it was several months. When one of the plants was shut down we had to do distasteful tasks such as change bubble caps in a fractionating tower. It was cold, wet, dirty, work often done on the night shift, because when a unit was down there were three shifts around the clock until it was ready to go on line again. Digging in a nice clean ditch on day shift was much to be preferred, at least by me. However, I remember Dick and I digging up a pipe line one day, and he said,

"Souce are you sure that this is what we want to do for a living?" Another time we just arrived at the Labor Shack after a hard day of work. Two busloads of students from the University of California at Berkeley were loading after visiting the Cat Cracker. Dick said,

"Their professor is pointing over here and telling them that if they don't attend to their studies they'll wind up like us." Most of the time, Dick could see the humor in a situation.

I was still living with Dick and Nadine, but since Phil Arezzi wasn't married we began to do things together. He was an excellent roller skater. There was a rink in Martinez, and he introduced me to girls he knew there. Neither of us owned an automobile so we would meet girls there and then take them for a snack at a local ice cream fountain. We decided to buy an automobile together, and he asked the family where he had room and board if I could live there, too. They said that if he was willing to share his room with me it would be agreeable to them.

We each paid $75 a month, and living there was great. We bought a 1942 Oldsmobile, and split the use of it. We often dated together, but there were other times when we preferred to date singly. By this time I had moved up to shift work as a Swamper at Number 3 Cracker. I wanted to get into the operations part of the refinery. The Swamper cleaned oil spills around the unit, and for things like vacation relief the Swamper was moved up to Operator number 5 at the Cat Cracker. The number 5 Operator read the charts on the control board every hour, and was responsible for doing some calculations related to the cracking of oil. Production went on 24 hours a day, of course. We worked eight-hour shifts, and ate on the job. There was a refrigerator and a steam heated griddle for cooking. The control room was spotless. The men were fine people with whom to work. In short, it was a very good job.

Thus the weeks and the months went by. I liked working at the refinery. Phil was a good friend, and the people we stayed with were kind. I was getting to know more people all the time, of course. There was usually a girl friend, but I didn't go with anyone for very long on a regular basis. I don't know why, all of them were nice to know. Occasionally there would be one who would "go all the way", but most of them drew the line for reasons that were important to them. There was no question in my mind about what I was after. If anyone was going to draw the line it had to be the girl, but I didn't force the issue if that was how she felt about it. Whether or not they did or they didn't, however, I would soon move on to another girl.

The life I was living was the way I had fantasized living when in the Navy. I came and went as I pleased. I didn't have to answer to anybody for how I spent the money I earned. I liked my job and the people with whom I worked. There were plenty of girls to date. There was nowhere near as much sex as I thought it would take to make life perfect, but I accepted that as being the way it was when you were single.

By this time I had become an Operator #5 at the Cat Cracker. Nevertheless, something seemed missing from my life. Occasionally, maybe as infrequently as once every few months, I'd get that strange feeling in my right hand. For a matter of four or five seconds there would be a quivering, unable to control it, kind of sensation, but it never interfered with anything I was doing, unless I happened to be writing at the moment. Then I'd pinch the muscle below the little finger with my left hand, and in a few seconds it would be all right, and I'd continue what I had been writing.

Every now and then I wrote to my mother, and she diligently answered with news from home. During the late winter of 1947 I began dating a girl whom I met roller-skating. Her name was Ann. She worked for a local Title Company, and lived with an older sister who was divorced. I don't know just what it was about Ann, but she was different. She didn't seem to care what people thought, including me. I dislike thinking I was attracted by that aspect of her. In any case, we dated regularly. I don't recall that we made any agreement not to date others, but that's the way it became. Now and then our date would end in a sexual relationship, but always on her terms, nowhere nearly as often as I would've liked. Often our personalities clashed. There would be a bitter argument, with neither of us giving an inch. The making up was fun, but the arguments were miserable. For the life of me I don't know why we kept dating.

When spring arrived the company for which she worked held a picnic for employees and their friends or families. Ann invited me. By then, of course, I had gotten to know some of the people with whom she worked, and it sounded as though it would be a fun day. The night before while on a date we got into one of our arguments. When I called for her the next day things were still strained between us. It felt very uncomfortable for me. She was kind of doing her own thing at the picnic, not ignoring me, but not paying a whole lot of attention either. Finally, I got her aside and said,

"Ann, this is dumb. We argue with each other when we could be having a good time. We've got the whole summer ahead of us. We could do things like go to Reno for a week end." (I was thinking about how there would be a whole bunch of sex on a weekend like that.) She looked me in the eye and said, "I'd rather go to get married." That's the first time that anything about marriage had come up in any of our conversations. I knew that she was kidding, so I went along with her bluff.

"O.K., I've got next weekend off," I answered "how about then?" She said,

"O.K." And that's how I got married!

There's not much I can say about that marriage to Ann. Don't misunderstand, there are many vivid memories, but there's not much to say. I notice that when speaking of the painful things my tendency is to speak only of that which makes me look good. We had three years of being together, and then separating for several weeks, and then getting back together. The times of separation were always initiated by Ann. It was kind of hell for both of us, I'm sure. If the most mature woman in the world had married me it couldn't have worked. I didn't have much more to offer than an erection and a steady job. We continued to have bitter arguments every now and then when living together.

The strange feeling in my right hand was happening with greater frequency. It got to a point where it was happening several times a day. No longer able to ignore it I reported to the doctor at the clinic, which the company had for its employees. After giving me a physical examination he sent me to a neurologist in San Francisco. The Neurologist sent me to Children's Hospital for an electroencephalogram. On the morning of my appointment, I had worked the graveyard shift, and had to leave almost as soon as I got home to get there in time.

When the company doctor received the report of the test results he told me that there was evidence of a lesion on the left side of my brain, and the recommendation was for a brain scan to be done. He said that they would tap my spine, and then take X-Rays of my brain to see what was happening in there. I had heard stories of people being crippled by that sort of thing, so I told the doctor I didn't want to do that.

After work one evening, while Ann was getting supper, I was reading the newspaper and had a very strange feeling. It frightened me and I tried to call out to Ann. No sound came. I could not speak. It lasted for several seconds, and when it passed I told Ann what had happened. I also told her that I was ready for the brain scan, and called the company doctor to make the necessary arrangements.

When I told him what had happened he had me admitted to the hospital in Martinez. I was placed on some kind of medication, and after a couple of days I was released. But I wasn't allowed to return to work since the tests were being scheduled at a San Francisco hospital.

As long as my memory works I will not forget that hospital stay. After the brain scan I had a severe headache. When I recovered from that I was told that they wanted to do another test. I had been given a general anesthetic before the brain scan, but for this one I had to be conscious. The doctor told me that they were going to put dye into an artery, and take more pictures of my skull. Just before injecting the dye he told that I would have a burning sensation in back of my face. That was an understatement. It wasn't exactly like a sudden blast from a blowtorch, but in that neighborhood. I had a burning sensation in back of my face, and then down to my genitals. A day or two went by, and nobody talked with me about what they had found. By then I was walking around. I saw the resident in the hall, so I asked him what they discovered. He replied that they had found no physical reason to explain the shaking hand, or the loss of speech that evening at home. He said that it was like a short circuit in my brain. Somewhere I had read that an epileptic seizure was like a short circuit, and I said that to him. He replied that what was going on in my body was a form of epilepsy called Jacksonian because it happened just on one side of the body. He also told me it was a condition that could be controlled by drugs that I would be taking the rest of my life.

He had no way of knowing, but had he told me that I had a tumor which was inoperable, and I would die in the next few months, that would have been easier for me to accept than what he had said about epilepsy.

When I was in grade school, there was a high school girl who had epileptic seizures. I didn't know her, but my oldest sister did. There was nothing to be done in those days to help a person having seizures. When such a thing was mentioned it was with a sense of shock in the speaker's voice. That high school girl hung herself, at the age of fifteen. I had skipped school one day, and another kid and I were going fishing. I was riding him to the pond on the cross bar of a bicycle. Suddenly he began to gasp loudly. I asked him what was the matter. He didn't reply, but he began to thrash so that when I stopped the bicycle he fell across it. He continued to gasp and his limbs were jerking uncontrollably. I was terrified. I couldn't believe that could happen to person. I hadn't even known that Ted suffered from epilepsy. When he recovered he was embarrassed. He didn't say much, just asked me to ride him home. The next time I saw him he asked me if he had hit me, or anything. He hadn't, but I knew that I would avoid Ted.

When the doctor told me I had a form of epilepsy I could picture myself getting to a place of foaming at the mouth, while thrashing around on the ground in front of other people. The medications, which the doctor had said I would need to take for the rest of my life were Dilantin and Phenobarbital. I religiously took the pills as prescribed, three times a day, but I told myself that the doctors didn't really know what they were talking about when it came to me having epilepsy. Those pills made me feel terrible, but the hand didn't shake anymore. After a couple of days at home I went back to work at the refinery.

During this period the voters of Contra Costa County approved the establishment of a Junior College. Because of the potential number of students it was decided to have two campuses, one of them in Martinez.

Several months after our daughter was born, Ann had gone back to work at the Title Company. We had one of our big arguments over that. I felt that Ann should be home with our daughter, Jo, she wanted to work, so that was that. As the junior College was being formed Ann thought she'd like a change so applied for a secretarial position with the college and was hired.

That summer of 1950 as preparations were being completed to begin classes in the fall we talked about the possibility of me going to school there under the G.I.Bill. I had been at the refinery for over three years, and had worked my way up to Operator #4. Ann had never liked me being on shift work, and she was quite supportive of me going to Jr. College. So I applied and was accepted.

Classes began in September. It had been nine years since I had been in the classroom. Back then I had hated it, but now it was different. My plan was to become a dentist. The only reason for that decision was that dentists were the highest paid professionals in the Bay Area.

My studies went well. The student body was given aptitude tests, and my counselor told me afterwards that my I.Q. was 144. That didn't mean much to me. He also said that some of the tests indicated that I was not cut out to be a dentist. He suggested that something in the teaching field would be more likely to give me vocational satisfaction. However, I had no desire to be a teacher, and dentists made a lot of money. I wasn't about to take his suggestion.

For those first semester classes: Chemistry A, Zoology, Creative Writing, Intermediate Algebra, Psychology, and Economics, I received straight A's. That gave me a great deal of satisfaction. I don't really know how Ann felt about it. Shortly after beginning the second semester she told me that she didn't care to be married to me anymore. That was the fourth time in three years. The other times we would separate for several weeks, and eventually get back together. This time, however, was different.

My old shipmate, Paul Wagner, had written me from Southern California that he was on his way back to Connecticut after trying to make it as a Fashion Designer in the Los Angeles area. I wrote telling him that my marriage was on the rocks, and asked him if I could go back with him. He was sorry to hear about the marriage breaking up, but was open to my going to Connecticut with him if that was what I wanted to do.

I was very tired of the roller coaster relationship with Ann. My feeling was that if I got away from there we'd be able to make a final break. Being with her had nothing to do with feelings of love. Nevertheless, it was difficult breaking the relationship. I dropped out of Jr. College. We sold our house, practically gave our furniture away, and split the proceeds. There was something like $700 for each of us. Paul came and stayed with us during those last days. There was no bitterness between Ann and I. We were past that. When it dawned upon her that I was going back to Connecticut she expressed some misgivings. The die was cast, however. Whatever there was of pain for either of us we brought upon ourselves. That little girl, though, was an innocent victim.

As I had back in 1944 when I had to leave home two days before Christmas, I did what I had to do. There was a huge empty feeling in my viscera as we drove away. There were three of us on the trip back to Connecticut. Howie had made the trip with Paul from New Britain, but they both decided that California was not for them.

In Nebraska we went off of the main Interstate in order to look up a Navy buddy. After the war, Paul Hedglin and his Dad bought and ran a tavern. Ponca was only twelve miles north of Route 20. It was early spring and we were soon hub deep in mud. During that twelve miles we had to be pulled out by farmers with tractors several times.

Hedge was glad to see us. It had been almost six years. He was married with a couple of small children, and another on the way. His wife, Joann was very gracious to us even though it had to be difficult to have Hedge come home with three strangers and no warning. Hedge's Dad had died and he was running the tavern alone. My impression was that he didn't like what he was doing, but only an impression. We stayed the night, with Wagner sleeping in the bathtub. It was his idea. We had a few drinks after dinner, and when it got to be bedtime, Wagner got into the tub. I guess Paul didn't want to be an extra burden for Joann figuring where we were going to sleep, so he got into the bathtub saying he just needed a blanket and a pillow.

There's not much else noteworthy about the trip. The Pennsylvania Highway Patrol stopped us at a roadblock and asked us what we had done with the pillows we had stolen from the motel. It was kind of tight for several minutes. Paul's car was a 1941 Oldsmobile with California license plates. They were looking for a 1941 Buick with California license plates. They searched the car before finally letting us go on our way.

My mother was no longer living in Collinsville. She had remarried, and she and Fred lived in a company owned house in Rocky Hill where Fred worked as a boiler fireman. Even though I hadn't written anything about Ann and I breaking up, she wasn't surprised to see me. Ann had called asking if I had arrived, and wanting me to get in touch with her.

At that time in my life I didn't know anything about anxiety or depression. I just assumed that the way I felt was the way that someone felt when unhappy. My intentions were to continue college, so I talked with a counselor at Trinity College in Hartford, and at the University at Storrs. With my lack of high school credits there didn't appear any chance to get into Trinity, but at the University I was told to take summer classes, and as long as I was able to handle the courses I would be allowed to enter in the fall. So I registered, and on the day classes began I drove to the campus, sitting on a bench for a time feeling miserable, and I knew that there was no way that I could handle college. So I drove back to Rocky Hill, and told my mother I just couldn't do it.

I went to work in Hartford at an envelope factory. My task required that I stand at a press, place a die on a ream of paper according to a pattern before me, and stamp out envelopes all day. The miserable feelings continued.

Along the way, I found my old girlfriend's telephone number in the Hartford directory. Naturally, I called her. She was surprised to hear from me, and agreed to see me. Her employment was with a steel company, and she stayed with a family in the city. I saw her two or three times and she was still the very nice girl I had dated after the war. I was able to tell her that I was sorry for the hurt I had caused her. She was very gracious about it, and didn't express any bitterness toward me.

I know now that I was very anxious and depressed during those weeks in Connecticut. It was probably a way of trying to deal with those feelings that led me to the decision to return to California, and face there what needed facing. I didn't have enough money to fly by coach so I called Dorothy and told her what I had to do and asked if she would loan me $100. She agreed. That night I told my mother and Fred. The next day I met Dorothy and Paul in Hartford. Dorothy gave me the money, and Paul drove me to the airport. He also took my car and said he would sell it for me.

Ann had agreed by telephone to meet me in Oakland. When my flight got in the next day she was waiting. She and Jo were living in Walnut Creek with the sister with whom she had been living when we got married. That afternoon Ann helped me find a guest cottage to rent within walking distance of downtown Walnut Creek. It took a week or two but through an employment agency, which was owned and operated by the mother of Ted Williams of the Red Sox, I got a job in the produce department of a grocery store. The fee was 25% of the first month's salary, so I needed to be very careful with money. However, being raised during the Depression, and through my mother's influence I was always responsible in meeting my obligations.

From something the manager of the store had said I got the impression that I was hired as a temporary clerk. The Post Office was just down the street, and I stopped there one day to ask if they were hiring. They took my application, and I had the feeling that was the last I would hear. However, one day a retired Navy Chief who worked at the P.O. came into the grocery store, and told me there was an opening. I began the following Monday. The fellow who had been carrying the mail on one of the two city routes was going to college, so I became a mail carrier. I liked the job. The people in the office were plain old everyday kind of people, with whom it was easy to get along.

Not only was that so, Ann and her sister lived on my route. I saw Jo regularly. Ann and I went out occasionally, but it was clear by then that it was through between us. She was dating regularly, and even talked of marrying one of the fellows.

The walk to the Post Office from the cottage was about half a mile. That isn't very far, but after walking my mail route each day it felt far. Not only that, but once a week I had to be at work at 3 A.M. to help weigh stacks of newspapers which were mailed to every address in the city. One day I asked a widow on my mail route if she would consider renting me a room with kitchen privileges.

She lived just a block from the Post office, and when she agreed my life was considerably easier.

Reading what I have written could lead one to think that my life was fairly well together by then. That's not how it was, however. I continued taking the pills prescribed. My hand had no further problems, but the pills themselves had me feeling terrible. Often I was so drowsy that I was in bed by 8:30, and even though I slept the sleep of the drugged I didn't waken refreshed. I took the pills after meals, and when I delivered mail my vision at times was blurred to the extent that reading names and addresses on the envelopes was difficult. There was nothing in my life, which gave me feelings of being glad. One day I happened to see one of the teachers from Junior College. We stopped and talked for a few minutes. He asked me why I didn't return to college. I told him that there was no way that I could do that.

Deciding to try and tie up loose ends in my life, I spoke with an attorney on my mail route about getting a divorce from Ann. After hearing my story he said that he would be glad to take care of it. That evening I told Ann. She agreed that we needed to do that, and she asked if I would allow her to be the one to get the divorce. Her feeling was that it would look strange to people she knew and worked with if I divorced her. I replied that if she got the divorce I would look like the villain. Her response was that since I had no family in California it didn't matter anywhere nearly as much what people thought of me. I saw her point, so asked the attorney to get the divorce for Ann. He let me know that if he represented her he would not be able to represent my interests. I told him that I expected to pay child support, but that I wouldn't pay one cent of alimony. Ann and I had talked about that, and she agreed that was fair. So that's how it went. She was awarded an interlocutory decree with child support of 440 a month. My salary was around $60 a week, so I paid the attorney in installments as agreed upon, and the child support payments to Ann.

During that period Bob Baker's marriage broke up. He was one of Dick Gorgen's Navy friends while at Port Chicago during the war, who had met and married a girl from California. They had been living in San Francisco, and Bob having no place to go had moved in temporarily with Dick and Nadine. Dick was now working at the Post Office, and he asked me if there was any chance that Bob could live where I was staying. When I asked the lady who was renting me the room she said that if I shared the room with Bob he could stay there for the same rent she was charging me. I figured it was the least I could do for Dick, so that's how I got a roommate.

Bob and I got along fine. I had been asking for a transfer from mail carrier to window clerk, so when the Superintendent of Mails asked me if I knew of someone who would take my mail route, I asked Bob to apply. He was hired, and I began to work inside the post office.

Anxiety and depression were with me constantly, although those words weren't in my vocabulary, and I had no knowledge of either of these emotional afflictions. What I did know was that I felt frightened, and there weren't any happy feelings coming my way. One evening I read an article in the landlady's Reader's Digest about a new drug that helped relieve tension. It sounded like just what I needed, so I went to see a doctor the next day and asked him about it. We talked for several minutes, and he asked if I had ever thought about seeing a Psychiatrist. I hadn't, and when I told him that he suggested I make an appointment with one he knew with an office in Walnut Creek. Willing to try anything, I called and made an appointment.

IT was during this same period that I began "going to church". The phrase is in quotes for reasons I'll talk about later. You must understand that in my thinking there was a great deal of confusion. I don't think that any of the people I was around thought of me as being 'nuts', but I'm not positive of that. One of the thoughts I had was suicidal. It went,

"If the world is the way you've experienced it, Souce, then it really stinks, and you may as well quit." Out of that kind of thinking came the decision to see if I could discover something that would make life worth living. So, the decision to see a Psychiatrist, and the decision to "go to church" took place at the same time in my life, but were not otherwise related. I will tell of my sessions with the Psychiatrist first.

My first interview with him took place during an evening appointment. I had always had a great deal of respect for anyone in the medical profession. That sense of awe was even greater for one who was a Psychiatrist. He listened as I talked about myself, guiding the direction with an occasional question. It felt good to have someone seem interested in me. The fifty minutes flew by.

At the end of the session he said that he would be willing to work with me, seeing me once a week. Keep in mind that this was early 1952. Even so, Dr. Wasserman must have felt kindly toward a very confused mailman earning a little more than $60 a week and paying child support, because his fee was only $10 a session, although I have to admit, at the time $10 an hour seemed very high.

I do not recall exactly, but I saw him a total of seven or eight times. It was probably about the sixth time that he asked me what I would do in life if I could choose. That wasn't difficult to answer. I told him that I would choose to play baseball for the New York Giants. He smiled and said that given my lack of baseball experience it wouldn't be likely that I would get to do that, so what was second choice? Again, it wasn't a difficult thing to decide. If I wasn't able to play for the Giants, I thought the next best job would be to announce their games over the radio. Dr. Wasserman said whether or not I got to announce games for the Giants we couldn't know, but he asked what was preventing me from going into broadcasting, and becoming a sportscaster? When I said that I wouldn't even know where to begin he said,

"Before your appointment with me next week I want you to find out."

There were no radio stations in Walnut Creek, so I went to Pittsburg, and talked with the manager of the station there. When I asked how one went about getting a job in radio he told me that the thing to do would be to get work at a small station doing what ever was needed, and then work into being an announcer. He added that there were no openings at that station, but I should check stations down in the little valley towns like Sonora.

Dick had naturally been curious about what went on in my appointments with Dr. Wasserman. He got a kick out of me seeing a psychiatrist. I didn't tell him much, but there wasn't much really to tell. He had known about me going to Pittsburg to see how one went about getting into radio. When I told him what the station manager had said, he offered to drive me down to the station in Sonora on Sunday.

So he and Nadine and I went to Sonora and went to the radio station. There was only a disc jockey on duty. When I told him my story and what the fellow at the station in Pittsburg had said, he laughed. Our conversation took place in between the country music records he was playing. According to him the station manager had given me wrong information. He said that if I wanted to get into radio I would have to attend a school where I could get a Radio Engineer's license. With that license one could then get a job at a small station as disc jockey-engineer. He told me that the closest school he knew of was in Los Angeles, and that it took six months of training to get the license.

When I kept my appointment with Dr. Wasserman that week I was feeling that I had discovered a great deal, and I was looking forward to telling him. With a certain amount of pleasure I narrated the events, which had taken place in Pittsburg and Sonora. I expected him to approve my efforts, and it isn't exactly that he disapproved, but he said,

"Well, what have you done about enrolling in that school?" Somewhat taken aback, I replied that I hadn't done anything about that. When he asked why I hadn't, I told him that the thought of leaving Walnut Creek seemed impossible for me to manage. The thoughts were coming off the top of my head, because the truth was that leaving Walnut Creek, and going to Los Angeles had not even occurred to me as a live option. I mentioned that I had to keep my job at the Post Office in order to make the child support payments, and to do things like pay him for my appointments. He said that I could leave the worry of my paying him to him, and I replied that he couldn't take on the worry about the other obligations I had. His answer was that I had an appointment for the following week, but that if I hadn't made positive moves to get on with getting into radio he wouldn't see me again.

I felt kind of let down when I left that evening. Those appointments with Dr. Wasserman had been something positive in my life. It was good to have someone to talk to about whatever came up. I felt safe with him, and I felt considerably better than I had when I first went to him. I didn't want to discontinue. However, during the week I decided that I could not just pack up and go someplace else to get a radio engineer's license. I called Dr. Wasserman's office and cancelled my appointment.

During this period, as previously mentioned, I had been "going to church' each Sunday. There were two places of worship on my mail route right next to each other. Why I chose the one and not the other I do not know. The Presbyterian Church building was located on Locust Street then, just a couple of blocks from the Post Office. It was an old building, but well kept, and it was there I began to attend services. The sanctuary was full each Sunday. The pastor was a young man. (He was only a year older than I was, but I didn't know that, of course.) It was a refreshing experience. For the first time in my life I heard people laugh out loud during the sermon. There was a choir, which sang well, and I was impressed by how wholesome the people in the choir looked, especially the women. I left after the service, glad that I'd been thee, and determined to return the following Sunday.

As week followed week I had developed an internal commitment to give the church a chance, to make an honest effort to find out what it was all about. I would not now be able to speak of anything that was said in a sermon, but for the first time I was hearing things about God that did not seem Mickey Mouse to me. Something else I noticed was that each week during that period things arose, which could have easily gotten in the way of me attending services on Sunday. For instance, the Sunday that Dick and Nadine took me down to Sonora to the radio station it would have been so much easier to get an early start. They were living in Concord at the time, and not involved with any church group. However, I told Dick that I would be ready after church services, and he accepted that. Another week the landlady's car had died when she was visiting some friends in the next town on Saturday night. They gave her a ride home, and she asked me the next morning if I would go get the car for her. It would have been very easy to see to the car and skip worship. However, I didn't do that. I managed to do both.

One Sunday I noticed in the bulletin that a men's group met for Bible Study on Thursday evenings. The thought went through my mind that if I was serious about giving the church a chance I'd better begin finding out about the Bible. So that Thursday I went to the class. There were about twenty men of varying ages present. The minister was teacher. My vision was blurred from the pills I had taken after eating. When one of the men noticed that I didn't have a Bible he offered me his. I wouldn't have been able to read from it so I said, "No Thanks." I often wondered later on if he thought I was just unfriendly. In any case, it was a friendly atmosphere. The minister was an easy-going kind of person, there was give and take, and laughter along the way. The class finished at 9;00, and a couple of the men introduced themselves to me. One of them noticing the tattoo on my right forearm asked me if I had been in the Navy. When I told him that I had he said that he had, too, and added that he and his friend, Lee, who was talking with one of the others, had flown reconnaissance planes in the Pacific during the war. I was impressed! Navy pilots had saved our necks many times, and everyone knows that in order to fly in the Navy one has to be very sharp mentally and physically. That these men were involved in that Bible Study group communicated something very positive to me.

Ray Brooks was the ex-Navy Pilot who spoke to me that night. After we had talked for several minutes, the minister joined us. Ray introduced him to me as Pastor Upshaw. I didn't know the appropriate form of address. Back home the people always referred to the minister as Father Mayers. To me he had always been, Mr Mayers. The minister and I kept talking as the others left to go home. In the course of our conversation I referred to him as Reverend Upshaw. He grinned and said,

"The people around here call me Jim." I didn't have any clear thoughts about that at the time except that it felt good. This wasn't someone who was Lieutenant, or Captain, or Doctor, or Counselor, or Reverend, or Mister. There was no title holding me at arm's length. He was Jim! I was Souce! After several minutes we looked around, and the others had all gone. Jim said,

"If you don't have to leave right now let's go into my office, and we can sit while we talk." I sure didn't have to leave, so we went into his office. I don't have any recollection of what we talked about. After a while, Jim said that he had to get home, and then he asked if I had ever been to a prayer meeting. I had never even heard of a prayer meeting. He said,

"The reason I asked is that we have one here on Wednesday evenings, and I have some time after the meeting next Wednesday. I'd sure like to talk with you more, and get to know you better. If you can fit it in you could come to the prayer meeting, and then after it is over we could talk some more" That sounded good to me, so we agreed to that.

On Wednesday evening I showed up at the room where the prayer meeting was held. There were men and women present, most of them older. Only one or two of the men I recognized as having been at the Bible Study the previous Thursday. Jim Upshaw was leading the meeting, of course. He read a short passage from the Bible, and commented briefly upon it. There was then open discussion, and different people said some things about prayers that had been answered. Some spoke of what "Jesus", or "The Lord" had done in their lives, or in the life of someone they knew, that week. I began to feel uneasy. This was different than anything I had previously experienced. Not everybody spoke during this period, and after it became clear that people had said what they were going to, Jim asked if there were prayer requests. That opened things up again, and people took turns asking for prayer because of illness, or grief, or things like that. Then, Jim said with a smile,

"Let's remember these things as we go to the Lord in prayer." The people bowed their heads. It was quiet for a while, and the uneasy feeling in me increased. Then one of the men began to pray aloud. As he prayed he began to weep. When he finished another person prayed aloud. By then I was almost panic stricken. Never in all of my 25 years had I heard people carrying on like this. I wanted to leave. But two things kept me from doing that. I didn't want anyone to think badly of me, and I really did want to have the time with Jim afterward.

The prayer meeting finally came to a conclusion, people left, and Jim and I went upstairs to his office. The first thing he said was, "What did you think of it, Souce?"

"DO you know what the Holy Rollers are?" I asked. The only knowledge I had of that group was from having read "*Journeyman*" by Erskine Caldwell. Jim nodded in response to my question.

"Well, I'll bet that Holy Rollers would seem far less strange to those people at the prayer meeting than they would seem to me." I said. Jim laughed and replied,

"I know what you mean. I've had my own misgivings about prayer meetings." I don't know how this young minister, not long out of seminary, had the wisdom not to defend something like a prayer meeting. He could so easily have felt it necessary to take up the challenge, and when he did, make me feel as though I had said something dumb. Had he done so I suspect that is the last he would have seen of me. My tender ego would have felt attacked, and that would have been the end of my giving the church a chance.

However, fortunately for me that didn't happen. Jim accepted what I had said about prayer meetings, and we went on from there. We talked for a while, and something of what he was trying to say finally got through to my befuddled mind. I said,

"Do you mean if I say that I believe Jesus was the Son of God, and I'm willing to follow Him, that somehow His dying on a cross makes it possible for someone like me to have a different kind of life than I've known?"

"That's close enough," Jim replied. With my distorted value system at that stage in my life, I felt that anyone who said such a thing was a sissy, but on the other hand I really longed for a different kind of life than I had known. At the same time I was afraid that if I made that kind of commitment, faithfulness would require that I stop taking the pills that kept my hand from going dead. I was denying to myself that there was anything about me that was epileptic. At the same time, deep inside I had the fear of me thrashing around on the ground and foaming at the mouth if I didn't take the pills. I was faced with a dilemma.

Jim was sitting quietly on the other side of his desk while these thoughts were going through my mind. Finally I asked,

"If I had syphilis, and said that I was willing to become a follower of Jesus, I wouldn't have to stop taking penicillin would I?"

"Of course not," Jim answered.

"O.K." I replied, "I've said it."

"I'd like to commit this to God in prayer if it's all right with you," Jim said.

I nodded my assent, and that was the beginning of a life far different than I had known.

Oh, I do not mean that anything startling, or instant happened to me. Call it what you will, conversion experience, or being born again, or whatever, as far as I know you're the same person. All of the experiences that are part of who you have become are still there. Your nerve endings are the same. The things that frightened you before still frighten. The things that made you angry still make you angry. The things that turned you on still turn you on. There is a major difference, however. You now begin to live as though there is God. You are standing on the same spot, but you are facing in a different direction. You still walk one, sometimes very painful, step at a time. When that has been said, it needs to be added that I know what it is to be on the scrap heap of life, and I know what it is to be rescued from that.

In some ways I regressed to a stage in life from before I had joined the Navy. Bob, Dick, and I, each owned a horse and saddle. We kept them at a ranch outside of Martinez, and we spent much of our time riding through the foothills above the ranch house. We dressed in jeans and western boots, and wore big hats, and went to rodeos when close by. I went to church on Sunday and to the men's

Bible study group on Thursday evenings. After Bob moved in with me he did those things, too, and enjoyed them. He had a good disposition, and laughed easily. We were both playing 'cowboy' although neither of us thought of it in that way. Bob liked to read western stories, and sometimes he would read in the tub and get so interested that the water got cold. He said to me once,

"You sure learn a lot from these stories, like how to slip out of the saddle when you're shot."

I don't know why, but one day the landlady told me that she was going to have to raise our rent. When I told Bob, we decided to look for another place. Very fortunately there was an apartment available right on Main Street just about a block from where we were. It was an old building with stores below, and four apartments on the second floor. Even though the building was old, the apartments were clean. A fellow and his wife managed the building and had one of the apartments. I don't know how roomy there's was. Ours had a small kitchen with a gas range and a refrigerator, a living room with an old rug, a couch, and a bedroom with an old bed and springs. I'm very unclear about how it was decided, but Bob slept on the couch, and I got the bedroom. The couch was not only Bob's bed, we used its arms for our saddles. When Bob first moved in with me he had a convertible Chevrolet. After we got our horses he traded it in for a pick-up.

Not all at once, nor in a dramatic way, life began to be better for me. There were things worth doing. Quite often, Jim and Gwen had the two of us up for dinner. We both felt that to be a "wow" kind of thing. We were as sure as could be that there were many people who would have been delighted to be guests of their minister and his wife, and here they were having us. No need to say that the food there was much better than what we did for ourselves in the apartment. To top it off Gwen made delicious desserts. It says something fine about those two that Bob and I never felt out of place when we were around them.

Neither Bob nor I used alcohol as a way of dealing with life. The doctor had told me that I must avoid caffeine and alcoholic beverages. This was no hardship for me. I had stopped drinking coffee while in the Navy, and alcohol never led me to anything positive. I sure gave it a try in those Navy years, but I had the dumb idea that if one drink made me feel good, two were bound to make me feel better. What happened was that I would drink too much, and my body would rebel and throw it up. The people we were meeting through the church did not use alcohol, so it just was not part of our lives.

There were other things, however, that weren't as easy to set aside. I had become a member of the church, and most of the people we were meeting didn't use tobacco. Ray and Lu Brooks weren't members at that time, and Ray smoked a pipe, but he was in a minority. Bob and I smoked cigarettes heavily. When he wakened in the morning, and sometimes in the middle of the night, he would reach for a cigarette. I never did feel like smoking before I had something to eat, but I was using more than a pack a day. Nobody said so to me, but I had an impression that being a follower of Christ meant that one wouldn't use tobacco. When I mentioned that to Bob he laughed, and said that he liked to smoke, and he couldn't quit even if he wanted to. So I kept smoking, feeling vaguely guilty about it, but not making any move to change.

I still had the feeling that if there was an opportunity for sex a person would be a fool not to take it. There weren't many opportunities. After our divorce was final, which took a year at that time, Ann married again. Until that time we had gotten together now and then. We could not be married, but our sex relationship was fine. The man she married was in the Coast Guard, and they lived in San Francisco. I didn't see her or Jo after that.

Being a part time father was something I couldn't manage. It was easier for me to turn my back on that part of my life, although, of course I sent the support payment regularly.

A divorced woman, who was five years older than I, moved into one of the other apartments. There was a physical attraction between us, and we met a need in each other. There was nothing of romance connected with this. It was as if we were hungry, and shared a meal, no strings attached. Aside from that there was an occasional date with someone I would meet. Not having a car made that difficult, and there weren't all that many women my age around. Also, I felt that being divorced was a stigma.

While all this was going on, without him knowing it, Ray Brooks was teaching me about friendship. That may sound strange, but I honestly didn't know what it meant to be a friend to someone. On the ship we had a couple of sayings that sort of show what I tended to think. "Never give a friend the shirt off of your back. It just shows him where to put the knife." The other was, "When you've got a friend that is tried and true, screw him before he screws you." It would be untrue to say that I subscribed to that shipboard philosophy 100%. However, something of that was part of the way I looked at things. It is a way of trying to cope. If you suspect that the other person is likely to take advantage of you, and then they do, it doesn't hurt as badly. My experience up to this point had resulted in a healthy skepticism about people. It is healthy skepticism in me, I'm the one telling this story. Someone else would label it paranoia. At any rate, in my relationship with church people, Ray Brooks and others, I was seeing and hearing something different. This is what I mean: I was on my mail route one day about three weeks after beginning to attend the men's Bible Study Group. Ray Brooks pulled up alongside in his automobile. He rolled down the window, and after we had exchanged greetings he said,

"Something I've been thinking about, Souce. I know that you have a horse, and that you're without wheels. I've got an old Chevvy coupe that Lu uses to go to the store. My son, Dale calls it the Higgy Car. What I was thinking was that if there's a time when you'd like to go out and ride your horse, just go over to my house, and get the keys from Lu." I could not believe it. Here I had just met this fellow, and he was offering to let me use an automobile. I doubt that my feeling of surprise was evident, but I had a sense of amazement that stuck with me for days. I never did take Ray up on his offer. It wasn't necessary because Bob had the pick-up.

As often as not, we would stop at Dick's house on the way, and the three of us would ride together. Please don't misunderstand, I did not take Ray's offer lightly, and friendship began. He was a salesman. His schedule was such that he often stopped at the Post Office to see if I was ready for a break. We would go to a restaurant next door, and talk while having a bite to eat and a cigarette. Every now and then he would invite me over to dinner. He and Lu had two preschool boys, Dale and Gary. When it was bedtime Ray would put one of the boys on his shoulders, and I the other on mine. Much to their delight we'd give them a ride through the house, and then take them to their beds. After they were tucked in we would bow our heads and each of us say a prayer. It is still a rich, warm memory, hearing Dale in his prayer thanking God that "Souce could come over for friendlyship."

I said that Ray began to teach me about friendship. He never gave me a book to read on the subject. Nor did he give me any lectures about how to be a friend. He taught me about friendship by being a friend to me.

I became a member of the church on June l, 1952. There were classes held for new members conducted by one of the elders. There were nineteen people in the class. I don't have any idea of how the others felt about the classes, but they didn't have much meaning for me. It was one of the requirements so that's what I did. It is also required by the Presbyterian Church that those wishing to become members must appear before the Session, (the governing board of Elders.) This was part of what was necessary, and I approached these things as a way of keeping the rules. This says far more about me than it does the quality of what was intended. As for me, I had declared my desire to join the church to Jim, he told me what was required, and I was fulfilling that.

The Sunday we were received into membership, however, was not just a routine fulfilling of someone's requirements for me. It was special! During that part of the service, Jim called us forward, and addressed the following questions to us:

"In presenting yourselves here for membership
in the church, do you receive Jesus Christ
as your Lord and Saviour?"

"Are you willing to follow where he leads?"

"Will you be loyal members of the church,
diligent in worship and service, and will
You give of your substance to support her
Mission as God prospers you?"

I responded affirmatively to those questions, and I was serious, without much understanding of what I was promising. For instance, I had no idea of how much would be appropriate for a mailman earning a little over $60 a week to give to the church. Each Sunday I placed a dollar in the plate when it was passed. In all honesty I felt as though I was being generous. Oh, I didn't wave the dollar in the air so that everyone could see how benevolent I was, but neither did I hide it in shame. There was a question in my mind, however, because when we had appeared before the Session we each had been given a card on which it said, "In gratitude to God for what He has done and is doing in my life I will give $_____ this year for the support of the church's work." I knew, or at least thought I did, that God was doing some things in my life, positive things. Since that bleak time when I was thinking suicidal thoughts, life for me had improved considerably. What I didn't know was how much money I should give. By this time I had heard of the Biblical tithe, and ruled it out as a possibility for me. Yet, I wished to have integrity in becoming a church member. I don't mean to give the impression that this was a large constant worry, but it concerned me.

One day when I was delivering mail, Jim was in his yard. After greeting each other, and giving him his mail I told him of my dilemma. He didn't say anything for a few moments. The he said,

"When I come home after a day of work, my daughter, Midge is always glad to see me. When she hears me at the front door she comes running to greet me. I'm just as glad to see her, so I pick her up and give her a hug. Sometimes we get down on the rug, and go through some mock wrestling much to her delight. As often as not she has a soggy graham cracker in her hand, so I'll stop and ask her if she is going to give daddy a bite." Then he grinned and said,

"Souce, I don't really want a bite of that soggy old cracker, and I surely don't need it, I've got the whole box out in the kitchen. But I love that little girl and there are some important things I want her to learn about sharing in life. Don't you see, Souce," he added, "God doesn't need your soggy old dollar or your tithe, He's got the whole box out in the kitchen, but he loves you and he's got some things he wants you to learn about the right use of things in this world." That was a "WOW" sort of thing for me. My perspective was turned completely around from what I was doing for God as a generous mailman, to what God in his love had for me to learn. I don't recall how soon after that I began to give ten percent of my income, but it wasn't very long. It made sense to me that if God can be trusted with my life, he can surely be trusted with something like money.

That winter there was a ski weekend for the teen gang. Ray Brooks was going along to haul ski equipment in his pick-up. In addition he was a good skier and could provide adult supervision. He asked me to come along. It sounded as though it would be fun and I enjoyed being around Ray. So I made arrangements to get time off from the Post Office and rented some ski equipment. The week-end was held at Soda Springs, a ski area in the Sierras East of Sacramento. When we arrived it was early afternoon on Friday. After putting our gear in the lodge we went to the slopes for skiing, my first time on skis. Ray was no novice. He took me to the top of the chair lift, and went tearing down the mountain as if skis were his second means of transportation. I couldn't believe that anyone would deliberately point their skis down that incline. I got down by zigzagging back and forth across the slope, but I do not wish to mislead you. It was a survival thing for me. My path led almost directly across the hill. At the end of the zig I would purposefully fall, and lying down, point my skis back the way I had come with just a slight movement down. I don't know how long it took, but about half way down I caught up with Ray. He was trying hard not to laugh, unsuccessfully, but he deserves credit for trying. He kind of shepherded me the rest of the way down. After that he went up the chair lift without me. There was no way that I was going up there again.

That evening we had a good meal. To be sure, just about anything would've tasted good after that exercise in the high snow country. After the dishes were done we all met together as a group, and Jim led us in a kind of Bible study. He was a capable leader and the things he did, he did very well. That group of about 35 teenagers paid attention. We did some singing, too. I was impressed! Here were a group of teens singing churchy kind of songs, and singing as though they meant it.

After eating, and again after the meeting, Ray and I slipped outside for a smoke. We felt guilty about doing that, but neither of us was about to pass up the cigarette. Before going to bed we played a few games of ping-pong in an unheated recreation room. We were the only ones there. I am a competitor, it is in my nature, but Ray was able to beat me anyway.

That was a good weekend. Ray and I enjoyed the time together, and I was seeing a side of the church I never dreamed existed. Not only that, I was beginning to feel a little more steady on skis by the time we left for home.

The climate around Walnut Creek, California is such that often there are some days in February when it is warm enough to lie in the sun and tan. Up in the mountains, however, good skiing conditions sometimes last until May. A couple of weeks before Easter, Jim announced that the teen groups from Walnut Creek Presbyterian Church, and Fremont Presbyterian Church in Sacramento were going to hold an Easter Ski Conference at Zephyr Point Conference Grounds. He added that there was a need for two working counselors. I had no idea what he meant by a working counselor, but I was willing to find out. On the way out after the service I told him that I could get the week off from the Post Office if he could use me. He said,

"I can use you." I felt honored. My first experience of leadership!

The conference grounds are at Zephyr Cove on the south shore of Lake Tahoe. I had never seen the lake before. Nestled in the high Sierras at an elevation of 6,250 feet, the beauty of that setting can take your breath away. The conference center has dormitories, a mess hall, and a place for worship. After carrying my gear into the men's dorm, and choosing a bunk I found out from Jim what he meant by working counselor. I was mess cooking. I was proud of the fact that I had gone through thirty-nine months in the Navy without ever being a mess cook. Now here I was a member of the church for less than a year, and I was going to be peeling potatoes, and washing dishes for a group of hungry teenagers. Yet I was glad to be doing it.

The other working counselor from Walnut Creek was Ida Klick, a widow who cooked for the school district lunch program, and consequently had the week off. There were two women from Fremont Church who also worked in the kitchen. After the evening meal, and all those dishes were done, I joined the teens at their meeting in a conference room upstairs. There were close to seventy teens present. Jim, and the Youth Minister from Fremont, led the program. There were other adults from each of the two congregations as advisors. The day had begun early. I was sleepy, but I figured that those teens would be up all night. It didn't happen that way, however. After the meeting Jim told the group that we needed to get a good night of rest because there would be some heavy skiing the next afternoon. There was a snack, and lights were out at 10:00. The dorm was quiet. Those of us working in the kitchen had to rise earlier than the others so we had our own rooms. The women had to share, but I had a small room to myself. I slept like a log, and it seemed that the alarm went off instantly. When I reported to the kitchen it was still dark outside. Breakfast was at 7:30, and the day was clear and crisp. Ida and the other women knew their way around the kitchen, and the food was very good. After the meal was through, the minister from Fremont announced that there was to be an hour of silence immediately following for prayer and meditation. He suggested that if they didn't have a regular daily Bible study on their own that they read the passages suggested. He added that he knew this was a different experience for some, and that they would probably prefer getting together with someone to talk for the hour, but they were being asked to honor the desire of others to be quiet, and refrain from speaking to anyone until the clanging of the big bell outside the door signaled the end of the quiet time. This I had to witness. I figured that he was kidding himself if he thought that group of teens was going to be quiet for five minutes, let alone a whole hour. I wanted to be part of what went on, so I got a Bible from a nearby table. When they were dismissed there was no talking. The only sound was benches being pushed back as they got up from the tables, and ski boots clumping on the cement floor. I waited until the last of them were leaving, and I followed them outside. The early morning sun had cut the chill from the air. A gentle breeze whispered in the tall pines, and water of the lake was slapping against the dock that sheltered a summer swimming area. There was snow piled in shady areas where the sun didn't hit, and the whole area was strewn with huge boulders as if some ancient cataclysm had rained them over the ground. I stood there for several minutes taking it all in. Out on the dock, sitting apart from each other, there were three or four fellows and girls reading from their Bibles. I went looking for a place to be alone. As I rounded one of the huge boulders I saw an attractive young woman, dressed in ski clothes kneeling in prayer. I backed away, and went on in search of a secluded spot. Rounding another group of boulders, which gave promise of being a good spot, I came upon a husky young fellow also kneeling in prayer. I was touched. I knew neither of them, but she looked as though she could have been the belle of anyone's ball, and he looked as though he could play lineman on anyone's football team. I have never heard any voice from out of the air, either whispering or aloud, which I thought belonged to God, Nonetheless, at that moment I felt a presence, I felt communication.

That Easter conference was the first of several that I worked in the next few years. I continued to have some rebellious feelings against authority. That caused no problems in my relationship to the church, but it did lead me to resign my job at the Post Office.

That fall I got a job as school bus driver. It was a large school district. There were ten full time drivers, and some who drove only during the busiest hours. Each driver had his or her own routes to cover, and our schedules were precise in relation to time. The trips were arranged in such a way that on any particular run there were children only of the same age group. That made my task much easier than it would have been had there been a mixture of age groups in the bus at the same time.

I enjoyed the work, because I enjoyed the children. During the first part of the school year, the first and second graders were the noisiest. I think it had to do with their feeling anxious about school. I discovered that if I got them singing it was far more bearable than when each was emitting their own special noise. They went along with it, singing at the top of their voices. I taught them *Davey Crockett*, and *America The Beautiful*, and *Kawliga*. Those younger children were especially fun. I never knew what they would come up with. Perhaps I can illustrate. I attended the annual meeting of the congregation there in Walnut Creek. The meeting began with a potluck dinner. It was a very active congregation and there were people of all ages present. During the meeting cartoons were being shown to the younger children in another room. Some of the high school group had decided that those cartoons would be more fun than the meeting. I agreed, and we had slipped into that room. During the movies one of the children threw up. Someone turned on the lights and a girl named MaryAnn, who was a senior in high school, immediately took charge. She had someone take the child to his parents, and told the others to sit quietly while she cleaned up the mess. I was impressed! Also, I was very pleased that no one expected me to clean it up. I felt that women were much better suited for that sort of thing than I was. Somewhere, someone smiled.

My first run each morning was a full load of first and second graders. The very next morning as I was letting them off, a little boy said,

"Hey, Souce, someone threw-up on the seat back there." Immediately, the thought raced through my mind, "Oh No! Who am I going to get to clean it up? My next pickup was just two minutes away. By then another lad, wanting me to know what had happened, but not too sure of what my reaction would be, said, "Someone put something on the seat back there, Souce." That struck me funny.

"No kidding," I said, "Who did it?" He pointed to a boy in back of him and said,

"He did." As he got alongside me, I asked,

"What's the matter son, are you feeling bad?" With a serious look on his face he snorted,

"I don't feel near as bad as I did before I did it." That tickled me. I laughed and went into the custodian's shop, got some rags, and cleaned the seat.

I began driving a school bus September of 1953. Regular Sunday worship, teaching a church school class, Bible study with the men's group, and taking part in the Easter week snow conferences as an adviser were part of my life. Along the way I had decided that smoking cigarettes was inappropriate for me, so I stopped. Also, I had come to the conclusion that in the scheme of things it was planned that sex was something about which I must not be casual. Neither of these decisions was made in an easy way, nor was it easy to make that kind of change. However, I felt that I was being moved in a definite direction. As I previously said, there were no voices out of the sky telling me what to do, just a sense of being led.

Something else going on inside me loomed large in my thinking. There was a growing sense that there was more to life than being a mailman or a bus driver. Nothing the matter with those two occupations, but I was feeling that there was something more for me, and that getting more education was the direction to take. As I was thinking along those lines, however, immediate thoughts would come about how impossible it would be for me to go back to Junior College. I had passed the deadline for being eligible to use the G.I. Bill for educational purposes. There was the need to keep up with child support payments to Ann, as well as support myself while attending classes. I was 28 years old, and could not reasonably expect any help from my mother. The thought of where I could possibly get the kind of job that would allow me to attend classes was just about overwhelming. Two of the part time drivers were going to college, but they were living at home. Not only that, I had no reason to think that Mr. Degenhart, who was in charge of the transportation department of the school district, would even consider keeping me on as a part time driver. My problems with people in authority were very real, and Mr. Degenhart had no reason to like me. This kind of thinking was taking place in me through many weeks. I didn't talk about it with anybody except in prayer.

One day while driving the bus the thought went through my mind that if these feelings were the beckoning of God, then all of the concern about how I would make it was really an expression of distrust. That if God was part of what was going on in me then the thing to do was to go register at the Junior College, and deal with things as they came up. So that's what I did. I made an appointment with one of the counselors, Mr. Collins. He had been my counselor when I had previously been a student. His pleasure at seeing me was evident, and between us we decided upon a course of study leading to the Associate in Arts degree. That took place in December, so I had until the new semester began in February to deal with how I was going to support myself.

First of all it seemed as though I owed Mr. Degenhart a month's notice so that he could replace me. Bus Drivers aren't that difficult to fine, but in the middle of the school year it could pose a problem. So, after the Christmas-New Year break I went into his office, and told him that it was seeming to me I needed to get an education, and that I had enrolled at the Junior College to begin classes in February. His eyes lit up and he said,

"I think that is great! If you can arrange your classes between 9 A. M. and 3 P.M., I can give you four hours of driving a day." I was amazed. By being very careful, I would be able to manage. The job problem was solved. The feeling that I was being led was considerably enhanced.

I made another appointment with Mr. Collins. Driving a school bus until 9 in the morning and after 3 in the afternoon made it necessary for me to take some night classes. Between the two of us we decided on a general social science major. It seemed to me that teaching was something I would like to do, and Mr. Collins encouraged me in that. Since I didn't have a specific area of interest at that point, the generalized major made sense. It was an exciting time for me.

My schedule of classes, and the driving job worked out well. The thing of it was I enjoyed both my work and my studies. The choir director for the church decided to begin a men's choir to sing at the early service Sunday mornings. He asked Bob Baker and I if we would sing with the group. So we decided to give it a try. Neither of us liked being up in front of people, but the group was large enough so that we didn't feel conspicuous.

Singing with that group of men turned out to be very enjoyable. Practice was on Wednesday evenings, and sometimes a group of us played touch football in the street in front of the church building afterwards. It was dark, of course, but light from the street lamps enabled us to see just enough to play.

The semester was about half over when Bob told me that he was going to get married. This came as no surprise. For several months had been dating a woman who worked at the Safeway store. They hit it off well, and because of Bob she had become interested in the church. In as much as they were both divorced they decided to go to Reno for the ceremony. I was glad for Bob, but there was no way that I could afford the apartment while going to school. As I thought about what to do, Ida Klick came into my mind. Working with her at that snow conference had been a good experience. From conversations that went on in the kitchen I knew that her husband had died a few years before, and she had two sons in the Army. She was very active in the life of the church, and when our paths crossed she was always very cordial. So I called one evening and asked if I could talk with her. It was the first time I had been to her house. It was an attractive two-bedroom home. I told her of my dilemma, and said that in trying to figure out what to do, I had thought of her, wondering if she would consider taking me in as border, or renting me a bedroom with kitchen privileges. She was very nice as usual, and in the conversation that followed she said that she once had a border in her home, but had decided not to do that anymore. Then she added,

"But let me think about it. When do you have to know?" Rent for the apartment was not due for three weeks, and I told her that I had that long before I had to do something.

I never knew for sure, but I suspect that she asked Jim and Gwen what they thought. Several days after my talk with Ida, Jim and Gwen invited me over to dinner. Ida was there, also. Almost the full three weeks went by before I heard from her. She agreed to take me in as a border for $55 a month! That is one of the best things that ever happened to me.

I felt at home with Ida. She was a very good cook and I began discovering the pleasure there can be in eating a meal. As far back as memory goes, I ate for the purpose of filling the place down there when it felt empty. When I joined the Navy I weighed 121 pounds. At time of discharge, more than three years later, I weighed 133. I thought of myself as being wiry. It is perhaps more accurate to say that I was skinny. These nine years later as I began boarding with Ida my weight was still around 133.

As I got into the swing of being back at Junior College, even with Ida only charging me $55 a month, it became clear that it would be difficult making it financially. So I wrote to Ann, told her what I was doing, and asked if she would allow me to forego child support payments until I got the education I was seeking. In her reply she said that she would agree to that request if I would agree to Jo being adopted by her husband. That seemed to be a reasonable suggestion. I was not being a father to the child. In my reply I agreed to the arrangement. It made me indignant, however, when Ann wrote to tell me that I would have to pay the cost of the adoption. Not only didn't I have any money, I hated the thought that one day Jo would be told that I was so eager to stop being her father that I paid to have her adopted. Nevertheless, it seemed to me that my choices were very limited, so I agreed.

Being a college student was great. A whole new world was opening up to me. Being somewhat paranoid, it went through my mind that it was too good to be true, that life is such that something would come up to make it impossible for me to continue. It took me many years to learn the lesson taking place right then. There is a price to pay no matter what we do, or don't do. It was not without feelings of bitterness that I agreed to Ann's condition. Imagine my surprise one day as I walked from one class to another to be met by Ann. She said that she needed to talk with me so we went to her car in the parking lot. It was obvious that she was under stress. She told me that not only did her husband not want to adopt Jo, but he was insisting that Ann choose between him and Jo. She added that she loved him very much, and wondered if there was any way that I could take Jo, or arrange for someone to take her. I said that there was no way that I could manage to have her myself while going to college, but that I would see what I could arrange.

The only person I knew whom I felt free to ask was my sister, Pat. The only communication between us was through mom. For whatever the reasons, the siblings of my immediate family didn't write to each other. My mother was the go-between, and kept each of us informed of what the others were doing. My feeling was that Pat and her husband were probably good parents. They had three boys, and my mother's comments were all positive about that family. So I wrote to Pat and Jerry, and asked them if they would consider taking Jo. I received an immediate reply. Pat was ecstatic. She had long wanted a daughter, but they had decided not to keep trying. She wanted to know on what flight Jo would be arriving.

I called Ann and told her that my youngest sister and her husband would welcome Jo into their family. Her only comment was that Connecticut was awfully far away, and she'd have to get used to the idea. Jo being that far away seemed like a very good idea to me. I could picture a situation in which Ann and her husband would break up, and Ann would immediately want custody of Jo again. A couple of days later Ann once again met me outside a classroom. She said there was no way she could allow Jo to go that far away. She added that her sister, Pat had agreed to take Jo.

I liked Ann's sister, Pat. She and her husband, Royal, had been married during W II. He ran his own butcher shop in a Martinez grocery store. They owned their own home, and when they discovered that they were unable to have children they adopted a boy who was just a year older than Jo. I was disappointed that my sister wouldn't be adding Jo to her family, but there was no way that I could object to Pat and Terry. I still had the feeling that Jo was in the middle, being bounced around, and if something happened to Ann's marriage she would want to have Jo back. So I said that the only way I would agree to the arrangement was if Pat and Terry adopted Jo. That is what finally happened.

The semester went by rapidly. My classes went well, and the driving job enabled me to get by all right. During that period I decided to stop taking the Dilantin and Phenobarbital. The drugs made me groggy, and when I no longer took them I felt much more alert. There was no shaking in my right hand. As the college year was winding down I was able to get a summer job as a lifeguard. One of the residential neighborhoods had a swimming pool, and the chairman of their committee hired me on condition that I obtain a senior life saving certificate from the Red Cross. Fortunately for me classes in life saving were held at the high school where I was bus driver, and I was able to earn the certificate.

That was a fun kind of summer! The pay wasn't all that great, but I was able to get by. My feelings of self worth had improved considerably. I even dated a couple of the neighborhood college girls who were home for the summer. Being divorced was a stigma in my mind, but they looked so sharp in their bathing suits I finally got up enough nerve to ask them out. It's a funny thing. I don't recall ever being turned down for a date. No doubt my memory is being very selective, and just refusing to remember something that would have been a let down. However, the point is that when I asked a girl for a date the answer was positive. Nevertheless, I don't think that I ever got around to asking a girl to go out with me, without having it all figured out that she would probably say "no thanks". I don't know if that is how it was with other fellows, but it is the way that I defended myself against rejection.

Being divorced, I say, was a stigma in my mind. Desirous that no one think I was trying to deceive them, very early in the first date I'd tell a girl about my being divorced. I like to think I did that without distorting the truth to make me look good. Much to my relief the fact that I was divorced didn't appear to bother any of the girls I took out. A major change in my way of relating to a date was that I no longer was trying to get them to bed. My ideas about women were changing drastically, and in my thinking, if a woman had a Christian commitment sexual intercourse was reserved for the marriage relationship.

Ida had taken a summer job cooking at Mt. Hermon, a church conference center located in the mountains near Santa Cruz. So I was on my own much of the time, taking care of her dog, Chipper, and getting my own meals. There were several fellows who were seniors in high school active in the church. I had gotten to know them at snow conferences, and through teaching a class of ninth graders. Sometimes we would go to a movie together, or swimming. Even though I was a veteran, divorced, and almost twelve years older than they were, they accepted me like one of the gang. It was as if I had gone back to my teen years, and begun growing from there. I still had problems. As it is for others, I was blissfully unaware of that, and all in all it was a grand time in my life.

When fall arrived I was eager to begin college classes again. There was a new head of the bus pool. Mr. Degenhart had gone on to something else, and a retired captain from the California Highway Patrol had taken the job. There was no problem about getting my job back. Maybe I was beginning to mellow in relation to authority, or maybe the captain knew how to deal with fellows like me. In any case, we got along well. Driving for him was a pleasure.

One of my classes was Humanities IA. It created a hunger in me to know more. That's the "whole new world" that was opening up for me. I had the feeling that this was an area in which I would enjoy teaching one day. History was another subject I enjoyed. Speech IA boosted anxiety feelings in me to a new high. Being in front of the class to give a speech was difficult, but I don't think I let that show. I knew that if I was ever to be a teacher the feeling couldn't be allowed to control my life. It may be that I was only fooling myself about my anxiety not showing. Something, which affirms the impression that I handled it well was the speech teacher, Miss Whitcomb, asking me to take one of the parts in the spring drama. The play was *"Home Of the Brave"*. The part she asked me to do was Mingo, a sergeant in the Army during WW II. Deciding that my Navy experience was good training, and not without some ego involved, I took the part. It was quite a move for someone who didn't like being up in front of people.

I continued to teach the ninth grade boy's class in the church school. Ray Brooks was superintendent, and our friendship continued to grow. Early in the fall thee was a Saturday afternoon meeting for the church school faculty. A student from San Anselmo Seminary was doing field-work with the Walnut Creek congregation, and since Christian Education was his area he was in charge of the meeting. I met Chrissie that day. She was a college girl taking a year out from classes in order to earn the money to take her junior year abroad in Lebanon. There is no way that I could exaggerate how impressed I was with that young woman.

I do not recall now how long it took for me to ask Chrissie for a date, but it took a while for me to get up enough nerve. It may be that I had dated a girl who was a professing Christian before in my life. If so I didn't know it. Nothing about the Church, or God, or being a follower of Christ, was part of any conversation I had with a date in those other years. Her Christian commitment was central for Chris. The friendship that developed between us was special for me. I like to think that she enjoyed knowing me, too. Chris was a highlight of that second college year. I very gladly would have gotten serious about her, but she had other priorities.

Ray Ferro, one of the other part time bus drivers, was a student at the University Of California in Berkeley. We got along together well. Now and then, after our afternoon runs were complete, we would sit for a while in his car listening to Don Sherwood, a San Francisco disc jockey on K.S.F.O. Ray was studying to be a school administrator, and encouraged me to register at the University, giving me the name of his counselor. So I decided to begin the process.

Ray was a member of Sigma Nu fraternity. He was able to get me into all of the home football games that fall, and some of the basketball games that winter. That was the time of Jackie Jensen, Pete Schabarum, Jim Monachino, and Bob Solari in football, and Pete Newell as head coach in basketball. It was a good time for the University in athletic competition. After the Homecoming Game with U.C.L.A. Ray brought me to his Fraternity House where Bob Scobi and his band were playing Dixieland. I met some of Ray's friends, of course. My interest in attending Cal grew by leaps and bounds.

The part of Mingo in the spring drama was not easy for me to do, but I was glad that I had accepted the role. Miss Whitcomb, was a good director. It was obvious that she enjoyed drama, and she demanded and got the best from her actors. At times we were in conflict, my problem with authority. I felt that she got carried away occasionally, and she may have rued the day she asked me to act. *Home of the Brave* played for two nights at the Junior College. It was a good experience, and those of us in the drama received many strokes for the job we did. Graduation was the last time I saw any of the four who were in the play with me, but I remember them well. Life has a way of doing that to us. We brush against another person for a short time, and then our paths go in different directions, and we see them no more. So much of my life has been saying "good-bye" to people when I would much rather be saying "hello".

My application to enter the University had some difficulty. I had never taken Geometry. My three semesters of work at the Junior College had resulted in a good grade point average, and that was in my favor. The counselor said that if my fourth semester grades were as good she would then take my application before a committee, and ask that I be allowed to enter without the Geometry. Just the possibility of attending the University gave my ego a boost.

Chrissie and I were both counselors for the high school group's Easter Ski Conference. I drove a rented truck with all of the sleeping bags, luggage, and ski equipment. Chris rode with me. Ray Ferro and I used to joke about a blissful marriage being Cloud 9. Chrissie and I didn't talk marriage, but there were times when she made me feel as though I must be on cloud 8. Then she would begin to wonder if we should date as much, or if I should drive all the way over to her house on a Sunday to take her to worship services. When something like that came up I was going down past those clouds so rapidly I couldn't see the numbers as I went by. The Ski Conference was one of those descending times.

The youth Group had grown so large by this time that Jim no longer could handle everything. The main speaker was brought in from Young Life, a Christian ministry aimed at high school students. He was an excellent speaker. I enjoyed being with the people in that high school group. When the conference was over I was feeling that I would like to work in a church related vocation. It was just a general kind of feeling, nothing specific.

A few weeks later, after my last class of the day, I was on my way over to make my afternoon bus runs. Jim's house was on my way, and since I had a bit of extra time I knocked on his door to see if he was home. He was there alone, had just gotten there himself to change his shirt before attending a meeting. I stood in the door of his bedroom, and we passed the time of day while he changed. For the first time I saw a picture of his seminary class hanging on the wall. I had known for some time that he had graduated from seminary at Princeton in New Jersey, but never having been in his bedroom I had not seen the picture before. Many of the men in the picture were obviously older than Jim. I commented upon that, and asked him about it. He replied that he didn't know for sure, but had an opinion that some people tried other things for about nine years before recognizing that God was beckoning them into the ministry.

As I was driving the school bus that afternoon I thought about what Jim had said. Teaching in the Humanities was no longer interesting for me. Because of conflict with my bus schedule I had to take the 2nd semester class at night. Not only so, the study had moved to more modern times, and was nowhere nearly as interesting as when it had been on ancient Greece. It went through my mind that I could spend the next several years trying to discover something interesting enough to lead to a major area of study so that I would enjoy teaching in that area. Already thirty years old, I didn't feel as though I had that kind of time. Then I thought that if I began to move in the direction of ministry in the church, and that was the wrong way to go, God would be able to close that door real quickly. It felt like good solid thinking to me, and that is how I decided to study to become a minister. This was another occasion when I felt as though I was being led, even thought there was no audible voice speaking to me. One day soon after that I stopped by and told Jim my thinking. He said, "I'm not surprised." He didn't say much more than that, but I felt supported in what I was thinking.

The decision to study for the ministry changed my thinking about attending the University of California. There were several students from the congregation enrolled at Whitworth College in Spokane, Washington. Chrissie had taken her first two years there, and spoke warmly of the experience. Whitworth is one of more than thirty institutions of higher learning related to the Presbyterian Church. For someone raised in a church environment the campus of a State University may be just the experience needed. However, with my background it was seeming to me that I would benefit most from a Church related college. So I began the application process in the few weeks before graduating from Junior College.

In response to my letter, the Director of Admissions sent me a college brochure. In his covering letter he encouraged me to get my application in as soon as possible since I was beginning late, and the number of students they could accept was limited. So I went about getting the necessary transcript of my work at the Junior College, and the letters of recommendation required. It was very exciting for me, a special time in my life.

By nature I am a worrier, I think the disposition to worry came with my genes and chromosomes. Without really knowing for sure, I suspect that is how my last name was derived. The Soucy family tree goes back to a village not far from Paris. My guess is that the name is related to the French word 'souci'. The word means "care" or "worry". You're acquainted with the French phrase, sans souci, and it's meaning, "without care". I'm guessing that back before people had last names there was a man in that village outside of Paris whom the other villagers referred to as, 'souci', because he was filled with care, "the worrier".

Well, that is all guesswork. However it came about I am a worrier.

I had no idea how I would be able to bear the cost of Whitworth. Strangely, I wasn't worried about that. Several weeks before classes were through for the summer I had applied at the refinery for a summer job. College students had been hired as vacation relief when I worked there, and I hoped that was still the practice. My previous experience helped, as did knowing some of the men. I was hired to work in the same part of the refinery I had worked before. The pay was good, but in three months I would not be able to save even close to the amount I needed to take care of expenses at Whitworth. Nevertheless, I was not worried. I had a sense of moving in response to beckoning, and that is a great feeling.

I graduated from Diablo Valley Junior College with honors. It was my first graduation, a very special time in my life. In addition I was given the Alumni Scholarship. On today's terms that $50 would not seem like much, but back then it was enough to purchase books for a whole semester. On top of all that I received word of my acceptance as a junior at Whitworth. All of their scholarship money had been allocated, and that was a minute disappointment, but there was too much good news to allow that to trouble my feelings about what I was doing, where I was headed, and how I was going to get there. All was not good news and glad tidings, however. Real life, at least for me, simply did not go that way. Chrissie had me going down past the clouds so fast I couldn't read the numbers as I went by. It wasn't that she didn't want to date now and then, just not as often as I would have liked. She thought it would be better if I dated other girls, so I did. They were all fine people, I enjoyed their company, but they weren't Chris.

As I look back on that relationship I have deep admiration and gratitude for the way her family treated me. Her mother and father, and two sisters were committed Christians. Joan, the oldest girl, was married to a Presbyterian minister. Her other sister lived at home, and worshipped with the University Presbyterian Church in Berkeley. Her Mom and Dad were very active in a Lafayette congregation. Those people were very gracious to me. That is unusual, or so it seems to me. Even though I was active in the Walnut Creek Church, I was a divorced man, the father of a child. Yet, if it was threatening to them for me to be dating their youngest daughter and sister, they never let on. They often had me over for Sunday dinner, and even loaned us their automobile several times when we were going into San Francisco. They could not have been nicer to me. Chris left for Lebanon a couple of weeks before I drove up to Whitworth. She didn't allow me to see her off at the airport, and that stung a little. We agreed to keep in touch with each other, however.

There were five other students from the Walnut Creek congregation attending Whitworth. Bob Gray, a sophomore, had been active in the high school group, and we had become friends. He was the youngest of three boys and was studying to be a minister. His Father was part of the management team for Shell Oil Company, and both of his parents were active in the Walnut Creek Church. One Saturday morning Bob and I were watching a baseball game on their T.V. set, and Mr. Gray said that he would like to see me privately before I left. So he took me into another room, and said, "Evelyn and I both think you're going to make it, and I want you to know that if you need money during the school year you can write me and I'll loan it to you." That was another of those "wow" kind of things for me! By then it was clear that I would be able to save a little over $150 that summer. Mr. & Mrs. Gray making that offer to stand in back of me with financial support if needed, greatly enhanced my sense of being led.

Attending Whitworth loomed very large in my mind. I even dreamed about it a couple of times that summer. My transportation was a 1941 Chevvy Coupe that I had purchased from the owner of a gas station on my mail route. It was a dandy little car, and Bob Gray had asked if he could ride up to Whitworth with me. I could not have been more fortunate. Not only did Bob know the best route to the college, after a year there as a student, he knew his way around. A personable young man, well liked by others he had been president of the student body in high school, and a varsity basketball player. At Whitworth he had made the varsity team his freshman year, no small feat. It would be difficult to imagine having a better introduction to my new college.

My thirtieth birthday was September 1. Ida had some friends over for a celebration. That lady was as kind to me as if I were her own son. It was a new world I was going into. Ida gave me a good send off and let me know that her home was my home as long as I needed it.

On the morning we left, I picked Bob up at his house. His folks saw us off with the kind of admonition that parents give their sons to be careful. After we had gone about 200 miles on the way we stopped the car and prayed together, offering the trip, and the school year ahead, to God. We didn't drive directly to the college. Bob had met a girl during his freshman year, and had made arrangements for us to stay overnight at her house, and then for Marilyn to ride the rest of the way with us. Marilyn's father was a Baptist minister in Alsea, Oregon, so we stopped there. As soon as I met her I could see why Bob had made the arrangement. Marilyn was a beautiful young woman. It soon became evident that she was just as nice inside. The trip to Spokane was a delight.

There must have been unconscious pressure upon me. Not many days after we arrived at the campus my right hand began to shake. It was just an occasional quivering for a few seconds, but it added to my concern. The financial problem had to be part of the anxiety. Even though Bob's parents had offered to lend me the necessary funds I was very reluctant to get into debt. That was my mother's influence. Money being very scarce during those Depression years was a very real part of my childhood. I'm grateful to my mother for the lesson. I've sometimes wished that, some of our leaders had been raised by her. Had they been I guarantee that we would not be in the financial straits in which we now find ourselves. If you cannot afford to pay cash for something, don't buy it. That lesson has served me well through the years.

Within a week of arriving at Whitworth I had gotten two part time jobs. One of them was as a school bus driver for a near-by school district, and the other was as custodian for a union office building in downtown Spokane. My pay from the two jobs averaged $2.50 an hour, and a little over $50 a week. The bus job fit in with my classes even though I really had to hustle to make my Greek class in the morning. The custodian job I could do a couple of hours in the evening, and on Saturday mornings. When I registered for classes, and was asked how I planned to pay I had given my $150 as down payment. I had then been given an application form for the Tuition Plan. A private company paid the costs of tuition, room and board to the college. It was much like a bank loan. The interest was reasonable, and with my two jobs I was able to handle the monthly payments with spending money left over.

That year at Whitworth was a great experience. While attending the Junior College I had the experience of commuting to classes. Now I discovered how much easier it was to live on campus. The long journey toward ordination had begun.

There is a great distance between a feeling that one is being drawn into the ministry of the Presbyterian Church, and finally becoming a candidate for ordination. An early step is in meeting with the ruling body (Session) of the congregation in which one is a member. This took place during the summer before heading up to Whitworth. At that meeting Jim introduced me to the Elders, all of whom I knew. I told them of my feeling that I was being moved in the direction of the ministry There was a time for questions, following which I was excused from the meeting. I waited in Jim's office. It never occurred to me that they would turn me down. Nevertheless, it was a relief when Jim came to tell me that I was now under care of the Session. That meant the Session had looked favorably upon my moving toward professional ministry, and would provide oversight of my preparation in the months ahead. I felt honored!

I wrote to Chrissie telling her of what was going on in college life, and my delight in being there. In her reply she said that my description of what it was like stirred her memory of her time at Whitworth, and she found that to be very distracting and she was afraid it would hurt what she was trying to do during her year abroad. As a consequence she felt it would be better if we didn't correspond. That was disappointing to me, but I honored her desire, and in the back of my mind kept a place reserved for Chris.

Through the influence of Bob Gray and his room-mate, Fred Bronkema, I became active in student government. Being dorm representative on the student council was very enjoyable. All in all it was a good year. I was able to handle my financial responsibilities quite well until the last two months of classes. The superintendent of the school district where I was driving bus made some changes that were causing me to be late for my Greek class. My problem with authority came to the surface in his office. I resigned the job on the spot, but I suspect that after what I said to him there was no way I was going to keep the job anyway. It made it necessary for me to write to Mr. Gray, and borrow enough money to make the last two payments on the loan for tuition. He sent it to me right away.

Before classes were out for the summer I wrote to the refinery in California, and applied for summer employment. They hired me. On top of that I received notice from the college of my being awarded a $250 scholarship for my senior year. As if that wasn't enough the Dean Of Students appointed me to be proctor of one of the men's dormitories. That meant my room and board would be free. Being older than the other students had its advantages. Those three things combined took much financial pressure off of me: the scholarship, not having to pay for room and board, and the good paying summer job at the refinery meant that I would not have to work off campus my senior year.

It was another good summer! Walnut Creek was growing rapidly. There were two health clubs in town. Three of us signed up at one of them run by a fellow named Bob Kellog. Ray Williamson, a student at Stanford, Gary Howerton, a recent graduate of Junior College, and I, worked out in a supervised program all that summer. Bob Kellog gave to each of us a schedule of weight lifting and other exercises, which we followed four to six times a week. The muscles really complained when we began. At least mine did. Gary and Ray were both active in the athletic programs of their respective schools, and this was their way of keeping in shape during the summer months. By the end of summer I was in the best physical condition of my life.

I don't recall doing any dating that summer.

From somewhere I heard that Chris had gotten engaged to an American student who was studying in Lebanon, also. They were staying another year to complete college there. Somehow I was beginning to form the opinion that I had no place in Chrissie's future. My not dating was in no way playing the role of the forlorn lover, however. There just weren't any young women around in whom I was interested.

The Session of the Walnut Creek Church recommended to San Francisco Presbytery that I be taken under care of the Presbytery as a candidate for the Gospel Ministry. This meant several meetings with the Presbytery's committee, which had responsibility for that aspect of the Presbytery's work. The committee was made up of several ministers and lay elders. They talked with me about what it was that led me to believe that the ministry of the church was for me. They also asked about my academic work. Following that first meeting it was arranged for me to take several psychological tests, two of which I recall: the Minnesota Multi-Phasic Test, and a Thematic Apperception Test. The first required answering a series of about 900 questions. For the second, I was given a series of 15 cards. On 14 of the cards there were pictures about which I was instructed to write a brief explanation of what I thought each picture portrayed. The last card was blank, and I was supposed to imagine a picture and write about that.

It took someone a while to rate the tests. Then I received word to meet with a Psychiatrist who was affiliated with Presbytery. He had my test results, and talked with me for about an hour. My only recollection of our conversation was his wondering if I had considered teaching in one of the social sciences since the tests indicated strengths in that direction. I related to him the thinking that had led me to where I was. It must have been acceptable, because at my next meeting with the Candidate's Committee they voted to recommend to Presbytery that I be taken under care as a candidate for the ministry.

Bob Gray bought his first automobile that summer. So I rode back to Whitworth with him. We had arranged to be roommates, and were both on the Welcoming Committee. That meant we had to arrive at the college a week early. The main task we had was to greet incoming Freshmen, and help them feel at home. For the first time in its history the college had decided to have a bus for things like ski trips to Mt. Spokane, or a choir concert in Spokane, or making it possible for nursing students residing at Deaconess Hospital to take part in evening events held on campus. Since I had the necessary license I got the job of bus driver. It paid me $1 an hour, as did a job cleaning the art lab evenings. It didn't amount to a large number of hours worked, but those two jobs provided spending money.

Bob was a dandy roommate. His sense of humor was refreshing, and we had many good laughs together. A person would really have to work at not getting along with him. He and Marilyn saw a lot of each other. One snowy evening they were parked in back of the campus, and when it came time to return to the dorm the car was stuck. The next day was Saturday, and Bob asked if I would come out and help him get his car unstuck. He said to give him a few minutes to get the car warmed up, and then we could shovel it out together. It had been a good storm, and the snow was knee deep. Taking him at his word I waited a while before putting on jacket, gloves and overshoes, and walking out to where the car was stuck. He was cleaning snow off of the windshield as I drew near. I said,

"Hey, mister did you happen to see a group of people stranded out here in the snow?" He looked at me with a sly grin and burped.

"They didn't happen to be the Donner Party did they," he asked?.

I dated every now and then. There were so many fine young women in the student body. I even became semi-serious with one of them to the point of dating her only. Then one night after a date I thought to myself, "What the heck am I doing?" Thereafter, I cooled that relationship, and began dating others. During the spring Bob and Marilyn announced their engagement. They told me of their plans to get married on campus close to the end of the semester, and asked me to be in the wedding party. What a fine couple they made! I don't know of anyone who didn't hold them in high regard.

Most of the ministerial students on campus planned to attend San Francisco Seminary at San Anselmo, California. However, there had never been any doubt in my mind about desiring to receive my seminary education at Princeton Seminary in New Jersey. The fact that Jim was a Princeton graduate had something to do with that I'm sure, although he never tried to influence me. A distinct impression from that period of my life was that graduates from Princeton were better preachers than were the graduates from other schools whom I had heard, and that seemed important to me, since leading in worship is so central in the life of the minister. In addition to those thoughts, the fact my family lived in Connecticut made attending seminary in New Jersey convenient for visiting them. If I was accepted by Princeton I would be able to see those people I hadn't seen for six years. That was part of the anticipation as I applied to the seminary. My life had been turned around since last I saw them. Consequently, when the letter arrived telling me I had been accepted for theological studies at Princeton it was special joy. There were many happy times during that last year at Whitworth. Far from the least of them was meeting Anne Creevey.

I first heard of Anne from Chrissie. They had been friends in the same class during the two years Chris had been a student at the college there in Spokane. Anne was a nursing student from Tacoma, and the two girls corresponded with each other after Chris left. When I decided to attend Whitworth, Chris gave me Anne's telephone number, and asked me to call her when I had the opportunity after settling in at the college. So one evening after returning from work at the union hall I placed the call.

We had a very pleasant conversation. Anne knew who I was since Chris had mentioned me in a letter or two. Anne had completed her nursing studies, was licensed by the State of Washington, and was working the evening shift at Deaconess. In the course of the conversation she told me that in a few weeks she was leaving for Princeton, to work in the hospital there. Her brother Bill was a third-year student at the seminary and he and his wife had suggested that it would be a good time for Anne to spend a year working and traveling in the East. It had been my hope to meet Anne in person before she left, but our paths never crossed. Well, that's not exactly so. One Saturday evening Bob Gray, his roommate Freddie, and I went to a restaurant for a late snack. As we were eating Freddie said,

"Darn, I forgot that you wanted to meet Anne Creevey. She just left here with her date." Although we did not meet, I did call her once more to wish her well on her trip. In back of my mind, no doubt, was the thought that Anne would write to Chrissie and tell her how nice and thoughtful I was. Whether or not she did that I never knew. In any case, even if she did it made no difference, because it wasn't long after that Chris wrote to tell me that she thought it better if we didn't correspond.

I gave no further thought to Anne during that year and a half at Whitworth. The beginning of my last semester I was standing in line outside the dining hall waiting for dinner to begin when one of the girls from Warren Hall introduced me to her new roommate, Anne Creevey. I could not have been more surprised. Truth really is stranger than fiction. Anne had become infected with hepatitis while at work in the Princeton Hospital. Quite ill, she had been hospitalized for five weeks. When she was well enough to be released, the realization struck her that she was far too weak to return to floor duty. Needing just one more semester to complete work for her Bachelor of Science degree, she had decided to return to college. So, against the odds that it would ever happen, I finally met Chrissie's friend, Anne.

During Easter vacation Bob and I returned to Walnut Creek. Three of the female students had made arrangements to ride with us. One of them was Anne Creevey. Chrissie was back from Lebanon, and had invited Anne to visit her during the spring break. It was during that trip I became aware of Anne as someone other than "Chrissie's friend". I began to see her as a person in her own right. Soon after we returned I invited Anne to see a movie with me.

Those last few weeks before graduation were busy. As the school year drew to a close my mother sent me a wristwatch in honor of me graduating from college. That really meant a lot to me. My sister Pat sent a card, and a check for $5 with instructions to "take your favorite girl out to dinner". There was no someone I thought of as a special girl. I was just beginning to know Anne. We had been together only a couple of times. Being with her was enjoyable so I invited her out to dinner with Pat's gift.

The college events surrounding graduation did not leave lasting memories. Other things stand out, however. A highlight of that period was the wedding of Bob and Marilyn. Freddie Bronkema made the trip from Princeton to be in the wedding party. Bob's brother, Don, a Presbyterian minister, was best man, Freddie and I were ushers. Mr. & Mrs. Gray arrived on campus for graduation, and the wedding, of course. It was a time in which joy was piled on top of joy.

One of my classmates, going to California to interview for a teaching position, had offered me transportation to Walnut Creek. The graduation ceremony was held in the morning. Our plan was to head for Walnut Creek that afternoon after we had eaten. I walked Anne back to her dorm, and we stood outside Warren Hall talking. That girl and I had not so much as held hands, but as I stood there I knew that I would like the opportunity to become better acquainted with her. As we were talking one of our classmates, Joanne Orr, on her way into the dorm said,

"Leave it up to old Souce, hustling right up to the last minute."

It was good to be in Walnut Creek for summer vacation. Being back at Ida's was like home, and working at the oil refinery paid well. Because of my experience I was able to work at my old job as a #4 operator for much of the summer as the regular workers took their vacations. The wages were excellent.

Upon parting that last day at Whitworth,

Anne and I had agreed to write during the summer. After getting settled I sent her a letter, and much to my delight she kept her end of the bargain by writing back. She had gone to work at Doctor's Hospital in Tacoma, and was living at home with her mother. I could tell that she enjoyed being there, but I was amazed at the poor salary that nurses were paid. On July fourth, a holiday, I received double time and a half for my shift. My regular wage was $22, so for the eight hours I received $55. That was almost what Anne received for a whole week.

Just before graduation I had received a letter from Jim congratulating me, and inviting me to preach at one of the Sunday Evening services early in the summer. That invitation came to me as an honor, my home church supporting me in my movement towards the professional ministry. I have no recollection of what I said that evening. Of one thing I'm pretty sure, what I said didn't amount to much. The people present for the service, however, didn't let on. They were very affirming. Jim and Gwen had me over for dessert after the service. As we ate, Jim said,

"Souce, you've got a lot of poise." That felt good. It had not been all that long ago I hadn't had much of anything let alone whatever it took to get up in front of people, and make believe that I had a sermon to preach. It must be something of benevolent grace that I was able to fool myself about that at the time. I actually thought it was appropriate for me to take the role of preacher in that service.

Those present were gracious enough to let me get away with it, the people of the church giving nurture to those studying for the ministry.

The summer went quickly. Somewhere I heard that Chris had broken her engagement, and was working at Mt. Hermon. By then I had gotten used to the idea that Chris and I were not meant to be. In one of her letters, Anne suggested that maybe I could go back to Princeton by way of Tacoma. It seemed like a good idea. Richie Johnson was going to M.I.T. so we planned to ride across country together in my 1941 Chevvy. Going by way of Tacoma was fine with him, so that became part of our plan. Imagine my surprise when on my birthday, Ida had a few people over for dinner, and Chris was one of them. When I took her home afterwards it kicked up memories of times we had dated. However, as we parked in front of her house, I knew that our paths were separate.

Rich and I drove straight through to Tacoma. The automobile threatened to boil over a couple of times on the way. We both began to wonder if it was a wise move to try and drive that old car all the way across country. When we arrived we got a room at the "Y" and got some sleep since we had been driving all night. That evening after getting something to eat Rich visited a friend while I visited Anne. Her mother's home was on a high hill, set back from the road. They had a breathtaking view of the valley below, and snow capped Mt. Rainier in the distance. Anne must have been watching for me. As I got out of the car she was waiting at the top of the stairs. The picture is engraved in my mind. The passage of time has not dimmed the memory of that good looking girl dressed in a black skirt and black and white striped blouse with a smile of welcome on her face.

The next day I took the Chevvy to a mechanic recommended by Anne's mother, Dorothy. After checking it over his suggestion was that it would be better not to risk driving the car across the country. So Richie made arrangements to fly to Massachusetts. With a bit of encouragement from Anne I decided to spend a few days in Tacoma, and then take the bus to Hartford and visit family before proceeding to Princeton.

Those three days were golden, nowhere nearly long enough. When Anne took me to the Greyhound station in Seattle, it was painful to leave. As the bus pulled away, I looked back at her waving good-bye, and knew inside that I would marry her if I had the opportunity. I had no idea how she would respond to that thought. We hadn't even come close to the topic. One thing we did do was agree to keep corresponding.

The ride across country was torture. If I had it to do over again I would get off at some town every evening, get a good night of sleep, and then continue the next day. It would have been more expensive, and I had to be very careful with money, but it would have saved much wear and tear on my body. By the third night my bottom ached so much I was kneeling in the seat part of the time. By the time I got to Hartford I was punchy with fatigue.

It had been over six years since I had seen any of my family. When I left Connecticut, early summer 1951, I was in a bad way. Now, September 1957, just past my thirty-second birthday, my life was quite different. I was in process: four years of college in back of me, under care of Presbytery as a candidate for the gospel ministry, and about to begin three years of seminary. Time went by rapidly, a sure sign that life was interesting, if not always fun.

Anne and I quickly got into the practice of writing each day. Nothing was ever said by way of planning to do that, we enjoyed hearing from each other, and it seemed the natural thing to do. As it got close to her birthday I began to think of asking her to marry me. When I was a mailman in Walnut Creek I had gotten acquainted with a fellow about my age who owned a jewelry store on Main Street. One day I had said to him,

"Phil, the time may come when I wish to ask someone to marry me. If that happens will you lend me a ring so that if she turns me down I can return it to you?" He laughed, and said,

"Sure, I'll lend you a ring." Anne's birthday is November 13, so I wrote to Phil, and said I was planning on asking a young woman to marry me, and was wondering about buying a ring. November 13 came and went and I didn't hear from Phil. Finally, the first part of December a package arrived with Phil's return address on it. Inside was a box with a beautiful engagement ring, and wedding band, and a note from Phil. He said that he had just purchased the stock of a jeweler going out of business for ten cents on a dollar, and that I could have the set for $26.

I knew nothing about Anne's finger size, but it made sense to me to ask her on Christmas Day. This is what happened. I knew that she was scheduled to work that holiday so that a married nurse would be able to have the day off. In our letters I had arranged to wake her on Christmas morning with a telephone call from Connecticut. I put the rings in a package to be opened Christmas morning. I included a bottle of White Shoulders perfume in case she didn't accept my proposal. In the package a letter was included should something happen and I was unable to get her on the telephone Christmas morning.

The seminary was closed for the holiday season, and I went to my mom's in Rocky Hill, Connecticut. The three-hour difference between Connecticut and Washington worked fine for me waking Anne with a telephone call as arranged. I placed the call at 9.A.M. and she quickly answered. After exchanging words of greeting, I asked,

"Will you marry me?"

"Yes", she responded. I hadn't thought beyond her answer, and I didn't know what else to say. It was such a big moment in our lives, and I was at a loss for words. In any case, she had to open her presents and get ready for work, so we managed to end the conversation. When she opened her present, she was pleasantly surprised she later told me. Added serendipity is that the rings fit perfectly.

We married in June. She worked at Princeton Hospital, and we lived on her salary of $295 a month during the next school year. Her mother sent us $25 a month and that really helped. We were in agreement that we wished to tithe our income as an expression of our being stewards of life under God. Strange to say, that made me ineligible for financial aid from the Seminary. Most of the students we knew, married and single, applied to the Seminary for financial assistance. In doing this it was necessary to present a copy of one's budget for the school year. When being interviewed by the assistant to the President, after looking over my budget, he said that if we were well enough off to tithe then he could not approve our receiving financial assistance from the Seminary. He said, "We think we are the church, too." I could understand it from his point of view, at the same time I would have thought that the Seminary would be first in encouraging the practice of tithing on the part of future ministers. One of my good friends received a grant from the Seminary. I guess she didn't tithe, but she did fly home to Seattle for Christmas vacation.

Each of the students was expected to do field work as a kind of on-the-job training. I worked with a congregation five miles from Princeton. I began that assignment with great expectation, even some excitement, at the thought of finally starting to learn some things about parish ministry. When I applied for the position of seminary-intern I mentioned several things to the pastor, which I thought would be helpful as he guided me. The only meeting of a Session I had ever attended was when I was taken under care back in Walnut Creek. The only funeral service I'd witnessed was at the age of eight. Mine was the only church wedding I'd been present for, and that one wasn't too clear in my memory. I still have no idea why, but that pastor never invited me to a Session meeting, or informed me of a funeral, or a wedding taking place that I could obseve. What he had me doing as preparation for the ministry was teach a sixth grade boy's Sunday School class, and then take part in the service of worship, usually the pastoral prayer. On Saturday afternoons the pastor expected me to call on residents of a new Mobile Home Park, and encourage them to worship at the Presbyterian

Church in Kingston. I disliked doing that very much, while at the same time I believed it was the thing that ministers were expected to do. One thing about it, that experience was influential, because it gave me the impression that field work was not likely to provide me with the kind of experience I desperately needed. As the school year got close to the end, the thought occurred to me that in just one more year I would be graduating, and hoping that a congregation somewhere would call me to be their pastor. Yet I felt unprepared in some basic things of pastoral ministry that any congregation has a right to expect from a professional.

Bob Hoag was assistant to the Dean in the office that directed students in fieldwork. When I was passing by one day I stopped in and told him of the frustration I was feeling from the sense of being very unprepared in basic skills for parish ministry. I asked what he thought about me taking a year away from the seminary, and doing work as a student intern in a parish somewhere. He replied that he thought it was a good idea, then reached into a file, and pulled out a stack of green forms and said,

"We have this many requests for students to do just what you're talking about." He glanced at the one on the top, and said,

"Here's a small Presbyterian congregation in Mound City, Missouri. They haven't had a pastor for three years, there is no response to their attempts to find a pastor, they feel discouraged, and they're asking for a student to be with them for a year to help build up their morale."

"Don't look any further", I said, "how do I go about applying for that?"

There is no need to go into the details, but that is how Anne and I came to spend thirteen months in Northwest Missouri. At this point I need to say that my experience as a Christian had been quite sheltered. By that I mean, the six years as part of the congregation in Walnut Creek up through Jr. College was a very affirming supportive period for me. Whitworth, and the two summers back in Walnut Creek continued that process. In its own way, the seminary was a special, affirming kind of environment. Consequently, as we thought about spending a year in Missouri, I had a very high view of church people. I had a strong conviction that the people of a church community would never take advantage, or lie, or be unkind to others. As part of that my concept of women had changed drastically, also. My contacts with females like Lu Brooks, Gwen Upshaw, Chrissie, and now Anne had nurtured in me very good feelings about women who had a Christian commitment. All this by way of illustrating that, not so much in my feelings about women, but in my feelings about church people I was somewhat naïve as we made arrangements to spend a year in Mound City.

After finals were completed we piled what we owned into our Plymouth, and headed west. It was an exciting time for both of us. In anticipation I was looking forward to a year in which the Presbyterians in Mound City would be glad about our being thee, and I would be getting the experience I needed to be a pastor.

The trip was enjoyable! We stayed overnight in Pittsburgh with Rea and Bobbie Weigel, seminary friends. In Columbus we visited a college buddy, John Scotford. Then, since Tom Sawyer was one of my childhood friends we made the rounds in Hannibal, Missouri. It came as a surprise to me that Anne had never read about Tom Sawyer or Huckleberry Finn. The visit to Hannibal stimulated her interest, and during our stay in Mound City she read both of the books.

Thirty years have gone by, but I still have a vivid memory of arriving in Mound City. It's about fifty miles north of St. Joseph, just thirty-five miles from the Iowa border. We drove up the main street to the bank where we were to meet Carson McCormack, president of the bank, and an elder of the church. Carson was obviously pleased to see us. He introduced us to everybody in the bank, then gave us a tour of the church building. That didn't take long since there was just a small sanctuary with a lean-to addition on the back end for a Sunday School class room. But the building was well kept both inside and outside. That was a relief to me. In so many villages across the land there are church buildings that are ugly, poorly kept, and in need of paint. I've often wondered what visitors from outer space would think if we took them on a tour of our town, showing them the places where we work, and buy groceries, and the homes in which we live. Then if we took them to the church building and said, "This is where we worship God." What would they conclude abut the kind of God we worship? The Presbyterians of Mound City would not need to feel embarrassed in such an instance. Their church building was well taken care of, even though they had not had their own pastor for three years. The Mound City congregation had been an aid receiving church for ten years. This means their resources were such that the Board OF National Missions gave them financial assistance when they had a pastor. There were only 65 members, many of them farmers, or retired. The annual income of the church was a little over $12,000. However, they took the responsibility for my remuneration: monthly salary of $225, $25 car allowance, plus housing. The church owned manse was rented to a local family, and it would have made no sense to evict them so that Anne and I would have a place to live for a year. A two room utility apartment was rented for us in an old brick building in the downtown area. It was a distinct improvement upon the apartment we had been renting in Princeton, especially for privacy.

Although there was to be no direct aid from the Board of National Mission, I was under their jurisdiction and responsible to them. At the Presbytery level, Al Devans, pastor of a newly forming congregation in the northern part of St. Joseph, was my immediate supervisor. Charlie Goodman, pastor of the Presbyterian congregation in the next town was the appointed moderator of the Session. Since I was not ordained, the polity of the church did not allow me to be moderator of the Session, administer the sacraments, or officiate at a wedding.

My responsibility to the National Board required a monthly report. This took a couple of hours to complete. I soon felt that no one looked at the report. After a few months I would include a question or two just to see if someone answered. None ever came. What can I say about Al Devans? He was a gentle man. Our contacts were positive, and when we met he was very supportive. We didn't meet often. My feeling is that he didn't want to stifle me by looking over my shoulder all the time. Not only that, it was a one hundred mile round trip, and he, like most pastors, was not afflicted with an abundance of spare time. Charlie Goodman was one of a kind. After the first Session meeting I said to him, "As long as these folks think of me as a student, they will never accept me seriously as their pastor. How about allowing me to moderate the Session?" He laughed and said, "That will be fine. It will save me a trip over here every month." There is probably not another pastor in the whole Presbyterian Church who would have agreed to that. It is one of those things that just is not done. Nevertheless, Charlie allowed it, and it was one of the key things that made my ministry to the congregation possible.

The people of the congregation in Mound City treated us fine. I soon developed a pattern for preparing to lead in worship. My mornings were spent in study, and writing pastoral prayer, and sermon preparation for the coming Sunday. Writing that prayer, and getting ready to preach took many hours. Appropriately so! I could recall sitting through the pastoral prayer with fellows from the high school group in Walnut Creek. It undoubtedly says more about me than it does the prayer, but my mind was soon wandering, unable to tune into all the things for which the pastor was praying. One of the teenagers usually timed the prayer, and I have a vivid memory of one of them whispering, "Can you believe seven minutes?"

I do not pretend to understand the relationship between the priest and God. It seems to me that unless the congregation is involved in the prayer when corporate worship is being offered, something is seriously lacking. The priest can pray from his room, and take all the time in the world. When others are present, however, it seems to me presumptuous for the priest to spend long periods in public prayer.

Somewhere I learned that we are able to concentrate intensively for about a minute. Prayer calls for intensive concentration. So I worked at writing short prayers.

I did not know what made for good preaching. Along the way I had gotten some personal ideas. Among these was the impression that good preaching is scarce. So scarce that if one is present when good preaching takes place, you long remember the experience. It was seeming to me that good preaching looks easy to do, it is never boring, and it leaves the hearer with a feeling that it concluded too soon. Those were my guidelines as I approached sermon preparation. One other thing, I had decided not to use notes. I had the feeling that if I couldn't look people in the eye and say what I had to say without looking at notes, it probably wasn't worth saying. This meant that after the sermon was written it took another four or five hours working upon the delivery. That process began there in Mound City. I've never regretted it. One of the things I think I learned from those folks is that people seldom hear what the preacher thinks he is saying.

One Sunday I had decided to preach about Stewardship. The main thing I wished to communicate was the idea that our life is a gift, and what we do with the gift says a whole lot about what we think of God and our fellow man, that in our life as the church we have the task of relating to the world in a sacrificial way. Being very specific, I said that I was going to ask the Session to adopt a goal of sending a dollar to be used in mission beyond our doorstep, for every two dollars we spent on what we did at home. That was the main body of the sermon. As introduction, I began by saying that there are towns and villages throughout this country in which, if it was physically possible to do so, you could go in at night, take the church buildings away, replace them with a meeting hall for the Eagles, or the Odd Fellows, or the American Legion, or the Rotary, or the Masons, and to all intents and purposes the life of the village would not noticeably be changed. I added that where this was true, the church hadn't existed there in the first place. That was the introduction. It took about a minute to say. The main body of the sermon took twelve to fifteen minutes.

After the service, I was greeting people at the door. When Mrs. Moore got to me she said, "You better lay off the Masons." My anxiety level shot up into the red. It amazed me that out of what I said someone heard me picking on the Masons. The next morning, Anne and I were just completing breakfast when someone knocked at our door. It was Marvin Heck with a basket full of vegetables from his garden. Marvin was a short, roly-poly, retired refrigeration engineer. His countenance looked like Grumpy of the Seven Dwarves. Inside he was soft as Jello. I invited him for a cup of coffee. While we were seated at the table it occurred to me that this would be a good opportunity to investigate further just how much of what I was trying to say in a sermon got through to people who were present. So after we had talked for a while, I said,

"Say Marvin, on the basis of that sermon I preached yesterday would you be willing for the Session to accept a goal of spending $1 for mission beyond our doorstep for every $2 we spend upon the local program" He thought for about fifteen seconds and then he said, "Well, no I wouldn't! We've got too much to do right here. I do agree with Mrs. Moore, though. You'd better lay off the Masons." So much for the efficacy of my preaching. That taught me to refrain from investing my sense of worth in whether people responded to my preaching, or not. However, something happened while in Mound City that was very painful for me.

Carson McCormack, the banker, was very enthusiastic about Anne and I being with the church. He went out of his way to make us feel welcome. Each Sunday, I could count on it, the McCormack family was there at worship. In the summer they often drove to Kansas City, 100 miles south, to attend the Starlight Theater on Saturday evening. No way was it possible for them to get back into town until well after midnight. Nevertheless, they never missed a Sunday. It was a high priority for them. Carson's wife, Elizabeth, told me once that if the kids were acting up during the week she would threaten that they wouldn't be able to attend worship on Sunday, and they would shape up as well as kids shape up. Amazing!

After we were in Mound City for several months Carson asked me what I thought about encouraging the people to pay for an addition to the church building. I mentioned to you that it was a small building with a sanctuary that could seat around 100 people, a lean-to room at the back for church school, and a basement large enough for the heating unit. Carson's idea was to make an addition which would include rest rooms, a kitchen, a multi-purpose room for meetings and fellowship, and a pastor's office. He said that he was drawing some plans to that effect. I appreciated his enthusiasm, didn't know what to do with it, and spent little thought upon his project. One Sunday after worship, a middle aged farmer and his wife who lived west of town, insisted upon giving Anne and I a ride to the apartment even though it was just two blocks from the church building. I didn't know how to take those two. He was the kind of person who readily spoke of the things he was against. Very early after our arrival in Mound City his wife had driven me around town pointing out where people of the congregation lived, and if there was any gossipy item about those folks she passed that on to me. I felt very uncomfortable with that, but didn't know how to handle it. I did not wish to offend her, and I didn't have the wisdom, or courage enough, to deal with the feeling that it would be better if she did not tell me things about folks so that I could get to know them without any bias.

On this particular Sunday, when we parked in front of our apartment, Wally asked,

"What do you think of this idea Carson has for an addition to the building?" I was surprised, because I had no idea that Carson's project was anything more than a kind of fantasy which he enjoyed thinking about for relaxation. My response to Wally was, "I haven't thought about it much. It seems like the kind of thing it would be well to place on a back burner and let simmer for a while." Wally chuckled and said, "That sounds like a good idea."

Well, time went by and Carson's project became more than a banker's fantasy. He drew up plans that were very well done, and gave evidence of a great deal of thought and work. I had no idea how a congregation went about deciding to do something like build an addition. From fellows at Presbytery I learned that thee was a fund available from which no interest loans could be made if the Presbytery approved a building project. Carson explained to the Session what he had in mind. It was decided to have a potluck supper at which the congregation could be informed of the proposal, and be given the opportunity to vote go or don't go. At my recommendation the presentation was to be put in such a way that if the congregation wished to build they would have to pledge the necessary amount one-third in cash, and the rest on a three-year pay off.

When the meeting was held, the congregation pledged the necessary funds on a three year basis, and a Building Committee was elected to function on behalf of the congregation. There was a good feeling, a sense of people sharing in a worthy task.

The following Saturday I went into the bank, and Carson's partner was there. Earl was a man getting close to retirement age with whom I shared a love for baseball. Unlike Carson, during the summer months there were many Sundays when Earl was not present for worship because he was in Kansas City watching the baseball game. On this particular Saturday Earl told me he had heard that people on the new Building Committee were talking about making improvements on the Sunday-School room at the back of the building. He said that the people he talked with during the week were enthusiastic about the new addition, and were obviously willing to back it up with their pledges, but he was afraid that if added improvements were brought up with the need for more money it would torpedo the whole project. There was another of those things I did not know how to handle. So what I did was get very anxious.

The task of leading a people in worship led to Saturday nights in which I did not sleep very soundly. With this added worry given me by Earl, I don't think I slept much at all. How grand if there had been someone to ask how to handle that sort of thing. I am sure that I could have called Al, but that never occurred to me. I guess I had the feeling that I had to solve my own problems. So, Sunday morning, after the Benediction, before people got up from where they were sitting, I stepped down from the pulpit and told them that something I had heard caused me to be concerned. I then went on to say that it had come to my attention that someone, or several someones, were talking about the possibility of making improvements upon the Sunday-School room. I added that such talk was really inappropriate because the congregation had approved the new addition, had appointed a committee to work on that project, and that if the people of the committee or anyone else tried to add to their work it would only do mischief among the people of the congregation. My anxiety level through all of this was in the red zone. As people filed past after the service Wally Bush gave me a dark look and did not offer to shake hands. The next morning I saw Earl entering the Post Office, so I made a point to see him. I asked him what he thought of what I said yesterday. He smiled and said that his son-in-law especially liked the sermon. I said, "No, I mean what I said at the end of the service." The smile left his face and he said, "Oh, I don't know about that. Wally and Ruth are really angry. They felt you kicked them in the shins." My anxiety level went further into the red.

It was my day off, but I felt that I had to deal with the problem. So I went up to the apartment, told Anne what had happened, and drove out to the Bush farm. The truth of the matter is that the Bush farm was the last place in the world that I cared to visit just then. Everything in me wished to avoid being in the presence of someone who was angry with me. At the same time, I believed that as the pastor it was my duty. Ruth met me at the door, and coldly asked me what I wanted. I told her that I had heard that she and Wally were upset by what I had said after the service, and I wished to talk with them about it. She invited me in, and called to Wally that I was there to see them. When he walked into the room, he looked as dark as a thundercloud about to cast lightning bolts in my direction. I greeted him and said that I had heard they were angry because of what I had said after the service of worship. He replied, "You son of a bitch, you think you're going to come here and change this town!" That didn't do a thing to relieve my anxiety. Nevertheless, I told them how information had come to me without any names being mentioned, and that I had no idea of whether or not it was true, but my feeling was that I had better nip such talk in the bud just in case. Neither of them warmed one degree by what I said. We talked some more with me doing most of the talking, I fear. When it was fairly clear that I had done what I could, I asked if they would be willing for me to pray before leaving. They both indicated that would be all right. (It is difficult to be against prayer.) After I had finished a short prayer asking for healing where there was hurt, Ruth said,

"I like to think that I am big enough to forgive and forget." That was the last Sunday that either of them were present for Sunday services while I was in Mound City. For me, their absence was like an accusation that I had failed. It says something about a serious crack in the structure of my being.

As I previously mentioned, up to that point I had led a fairly sheltered life as far as being a Christian goes. For the first five years the congregation in Walnut Creek, primarily people such as the Upshaws, the Brooks, Ida Klick, the Grays, and others, had given me a very positive impression of what the church is about. There was an implicit, at times explicit, approval made known to those of us studying for the ministry. The two years spent at Whitworth were golden. I function well in that kind of setting, and I became fairly well known on campus. Seminary was more difficult, but not therefore less supportive, so when we went to Mound City I had the idea that church people were basically kind and loving. It was traumatic for me to discover that is not always the case.

The days, and the weeks, and the months, went by. Anxiety about Wally and Ruth Bush was part of me. The episodes of a quivering hand became more frequent, so I went to Dr. Thompson, told him the history, and received a prescription for Dilantin and Phenobarbital. That took care of the hand, but the drugs made me feel terrible. One day we were at the Heck's garden. They were on vacation, and had encouraged us to help ourselves to the vegetables while they were gone. I felt so poorly that I mentioned to Anne how I felt, and said, "If this is the way it is going to be from here on I can't stand it."

Along the way, work had begun on the new addition. The loan was granted by the Presbytery, a contractor hired, and Marvin Heck was acting as congregational representative for the Session. In all that took place, I was getting the "on the job" training I needed. There were occasional funerals, and although these were times of great anxiety, I got through them. It was not unlike being thrown into the middle of the ocean to learn how to swim. If you were to go to Mound City, and have a conversation with anyone who had been part of the congregation that year, I suspect they would remember Anne and me in a positive way, anyone, except Wally and Ruth Bush that is.

One day, Carson McCormack's wife Elizabeth came to me with a copy of the Reader's Digest. She said that there was an article, "*Spiritual Healing*" that she felt I would be interested in. Her mother had died several months earlier, and I had conducted the funeral, the first funeral for me as pastor. As I mentioned earlier, the whole McCormack family was very supportive during the time we spent with them. That evening I read the article, and I was interested indeed. It was the condensation of a book written by Dr. Richard K. Young and Al Meiberg, both ordained Baptist pastors, about the work of the Department of Pastoral Care at the North Carolina Baptist Hospital in Winston-Salem, N.C. In the article it mentioned that ten interns from various denominations were received into the Department to take clinical training for a year. I talked about it with Anne, and told her I would like to apply for the year after graduating from Princeton. She was all for it. So I wrote to Dr. Young telling him something of myself, and my interest in doing an internship at the hospital. I received a response asking me for information, and telling me of tests that would be required. It was suggested that I make arrangements to visit the Department of Pastoral Care that fall before classes started at the Seminary. Those arrangements were made, and a date in early September was set for the visit.

We were scheduled to leave Mound City the end of July. As the time drew near, I encouraged the Session to call a congregational meeting for the purpose of electing a Pastor Seeking Committee. This was done, and the committee began the process that needs to be done when a pastor is being sought. One day Carson told me that he would arrange for me to have a new Ford, if I would agree to come back to Mound City, and be their pastor after graduating from Seminary. He meant well, but that kind of arrangement would have been inappropriate, and not allowed by the polity of the church. Not only that, the disapproval represented by the absence of Wally and Ruth each Sunday had me so anxious that I was looking forward to leaving. Carson also offered to give us a gas credit card to use until we got back to Princeton. That was a very generous offer, and we weren't exactly rolling in money. However. knowing Carson as I did, I was fairly sure that the credit card was charged to the bank, and would be written off as a business expense. Graciously, I hope, I thanked him, and said that it was important that we be responsible in paying our own way. The last Sunday in July arrived. I led in worship for the last time in Mound City. The next day we piled what we had into the Plymouth and headed west to visit with Anne's family, then go down to Walnut Creek to see Ida and church friends on our way back to Seminary, and the appointment in Winston-Salem.

The first night we stayed at a campground in Nebraska. While getting the campsite ready for our overnight stay, I had a sharp pain in my left lung, making it difficult to take in a deep breath. It went away after a bit. We ate supper, and crawled into our sleeping bags early. The Dilantin and Phenobarbital continued to work as far as my hand went, and in making me feel Zombilike. At least I am guessing that is how a Zombi feels. Nevertheless, it felt good to be on our way. We drove through Yellowstone, seeing old Faithful, and spending a night in the park. The rest of the trip was uneventful. It felt good to arrive in Seattle where Anne's brother Bill was assistant pastor at Woodland Park Presbyterian Church. We stayed with Bill and Gladys and their two preschool children, and visited with Anne's mom. Time flew, and soon it was time to go to Walnut Creek to see Ida, and the Brooks family, and others of the congregation. Labor Day soon arrived and we headed east.

Before classes began for the year, we drove down to Winston-Salem. I met with Dr. Young in his office and spent a couple of hours with his staff. Someone, usually Dr. Young, asked a question, or guided the direction of the conversation. It was a non-threatening situation and I answered as honestly as I could. In addition, I was given a battery of tests by the Hospital Psychologist. He was an affable man, and when he was through, he asked if we had eaten at the K and W Cafeteria while in town. When I said that we hadn't, he went on to say that it was a special place, and when in Winston-Salem it shouldn't be missed. He then went on to give me directions on how to get there. Feeling somewhat paranoid, I wondered if maybe he was saying that I hadn't passed the tests, and wouldn't be coming back to Winston-Salem, so I'd better visit the cafeteria while I had the chance. In spite of the drugs I was taking which accented paranoid feelings, I had the good sense not to mention my wondering. Before I left the hospital that day, Dr. Young told me that they chose the ten interns before seminary was through for the year, and that they would notify me sometime prior to graduation. That is difficult for me, because my nature is such that I want to know right now, or sooner.

When we got back to Princeton, it was a delight getting settled into our cottage. Thanks to a seminary friend we had known at Whitworth, we had a wonderful place to live. The Kingsford family lived several miles outside of Princeton on an estate with a four-room furnished cottage on the grounds. Mr. and Mrs. Kingsford had three children: Kathy, 14 years of age, Danny, 12 and away at Boarding School, and Michael who was 3. Both of the parents were away in the daytime on weekdays. There was a Cook, and a Nanny to take care of Michael during the day, but either Anne or I had the responsibility for putting Michael to bed. In addition, using an automobile of theirs it was my responsibility to drive Kathy to a private school on my way into seminary. For this we had the cottage rent-free. Michael was a delight, and putting him to bed at night a pleasure. Since

Anne worked the afternoon shift in the O.R. I was the one who put him to bed most of the time. I made up stories to tell him about an imaginary brother and sister his age, whose names were Pixie and Dixie.

It was refreshing to get back into the routine of classes. On campus, professors who knew me welcomed me back. One day Kent Kinney, Assistant to the Dean of Field Services, told me that a letter had been received from Al Devans regarding my work in Mound City, He added, "That's the kind of thing we like hearing about one of our students." In need of strokes, I would have liked reading what Al had said, but that wasn't offered to me.

One of my teachers, George Arthur Buttrick, was visiting lecturer in Homiletics. His classes were an inspiration to me. I wasn't alone in that feeling. After class one day, Charles Harwell said, "Almost he persuadeth me to be a preacher." One of my other classes that year was held at the New Jersey Neuro-Psychiatric Clinic. There we worked mainly with alcoholic patients. I do not recall the chaplain's name, but he was a good instructor.

In that fashion, the days, and weeks, and months went by. At Christmas time Anne and I went to Connecticut and spent the holiday with Fred and my mom. It was special. That spring I preached my senior sermon, as was required of each of us before graduation. Ernest Gordon, chaplain at the University, was the instructor for the preaching class, and very helpful.

While all this was taking place I got beyond the anxious feelings that had followed me from Mound City. I stopped taking the Phenobarbital and Dilantin. My hand acted normal. The end of April I received word that I had been accepted for the internship at Winston-Salem. Shortly before graduation I received a letter from Dr. Mackay, President of the seminary, telling me that I had been awarded second place for the Grier-Davis prize in Homiletics. A check was included. I felt honored, and so I should have. Ernest Gordon, must have liked what I did.

My mother took the train down from Connecticut, and stayed with us during graduation. She wasn't one for expressing emotion, but I could tell she was proud. Since we were not to head for Winston-Salem until the end of August, I talked with Mr. Kingsford, and he said it would work out fine with them for us to be there during the summer months. Also, I went to the Shopping Center, and talked with Hy about work at the Delicatessen. Since he was already well staffed, he could only give me part time work. Anne's monthly salary at the hospital was $295. We had been living on that through the school year. Her mom had been sending us $25 a month, and that came in very handy. I had received scholarship aid through the National Church. So we paid all of our obligations, including what I owed the seminary for tuition. Sometime during the summer, Anne received word from Baptist Hospital that she had a job, and her salary would be $310 a month. Several times during the summer, Freddie Bronkema invited me to conduct worship services at the Presbyterian Church in Atlantic Highlands while he was on vacation. I received $25 on each occasion.

Early June my youngest sister Pat called one day to tell us that Joan's husband, Bob, had died of a heart attack. I went up for the funeral. While there I invited their daughter, Joan Ellen, to spend a few days with us if she would like to visit. Her mom was now a widow at the age of 41 with five children; David, the oldest, was 19, Ronnie, the youngest was five. Bob, Joan Ellen, and Allen were in-between. In making the invitation to Joan Ellen, I thought it would possibly help her have something to look forward to. I have no idea if it helped in any way, but she did come for a week during the summer while on vacation from school.

When the time came for us to head south, we rented a small U-Haul Trailer to tow in back of the Plymouth. In our savings account as we drove away from Princeton we had $138. Our first order of business was to find a decent place to live. The cottage at Kingsford's had been great, and I think we were hoping to duplicate that. We found a place to camp, and the next day began our search. We did find a tiny cottage about five miles from the hospital, and rented it. It was good to get what little we owned unpacked, and the trailer off our hands. Anne began her work at the hospital, and I started my year as chaplain-intern. Only a few days went by, and we faced the fact that the cottage was a long way from what we had at Kingsford's. We easily decided that at the end of the month we would move. So we did. We went to a small downstairs apartment, rented to us by an older couple living upstairs. The apartment was only ten minutes from the hospital, a decided improvement! Mr. and Mrs. Baum were active in one of the local church congregations, Mr. Baum was minister of music.

The introduction phase of the program for interns lasted six weeks. There were books to read, the most important for me was, "*Client Centered Therapy*", by Carl Rogers. After an orientation tour of the hospital each of us was assigned an area where the patients were our responsibility. During that six-week period there was a requirement to write a verbatim account of a visit with a patient during each day. I don't know how the others handled that. What worked for me was to go to the chaplain-intern room in the basement while the conversation with a patient was fresh in my mind. Our room in the basement had a small desk for each of us. As you can readily appreciate, writing verbatims each day took time. Try it sometime. Right after you have a conversation with someone, sit down with pen and paper, and try to record exactly what each of you said.

Including Dr. Young, there were six members on the staff of the Department of Pastoral Care; Al Meiburg, Ben Patrick, Herb Zerof, Wesley Brett, and Charles Coglin. Coglin had the responsibility for reading those verbatims. Daily, the staff met with the interns, and one of the verbatims was the topic as a learning tool. These sessions were not judgemental in nature to show us how wrong we were, but to help us understand ourselves in our approach to ministry on behalf of a patient. Talk about the blind leading the blind, me offering pastoral care to a patient I mean.

The Department also conducted six-week classes on hospital ministry for pastors from all over that part of the South. The men participating were at the hospital Monday through Friday, returning to their parish for the weekend. Each of them was assigned patients to visit, and verbatims to write.

At 2:30 P.M. each day there were group meetings with a member of the staff. Each group had five of those pastors, and five interns. Herb Zerof was leader of the group to which I was assigned. These turned out to be group therapy sessions as we spoke of frustrations, and new insights gained, and becoming aware of wrinkles in our own personality make-up. I was entering a very important phase of my life!

Weekly, doctor interns, and chaplain interns, met in one of the hospital teaching theaters where Dr. Randolph, one of the staff Psychiatrists, conducted an interview with a hospital patient who had agreed to the session. After the interview, and the patient was taken back to his room, Dr. Randolph told the interns of his understanding of what was going on in the patient, and how this could be a factor in his illness.

So there you have a picture of our week. The day began at 8 AM, and ended at 4:30. There were five interns, who were in the hospital for half day on Saturday morning, so we had an afternoon off during the week. In addition we took turns being on call for 24 hours. If there was a death in the hospital, day or night, the on-call chaplain was notified. He went to the hospital to meet with the family. The staff physician usually waited for the chaplain to be there before informing the family of the death of a loved one. I should mention in passing, that not all physicians were in favor of the work of the chaplains as part of the hospital staff. Some didn't wait for the chaplain before notifying a family of a death. Even though it took me a matter of fifteen or twenty minutes to get to the hospital when called at night, a half hour at the most, there were times that the family had been notified, and had left the hospital before I arrived. Being called out at night was not one of my favorite things. One other duty was the responsibility for taking a turn conducting Sunday services in the hospital chapel.

The Department of Pastoral Care provided free counseling for anyone who contacted the department in search of help. After the six weeks of orientation those of us who were interns were the counselors. It was required that before becoming counselors, we had to meet with Ben Patrick. Ben was a very capable, well-trained counselor. The time I spent with him was golden. Not without tears, I worked through some of my unresolved feelings in relation to my father. When we concluded those sessions, I understood some things about myself far better. In addition, I was settling into the hospital routine, and growing in my understanding of ministry to hospital patients.

It takes skill and understanding to enter the hospital room as a stranger, introduce yourself as chaplain, and try to establish a relationship in which ministry becomes possible. Being ill diminishes one's confidence. The hospital routine tends to make one feel less like a person and more like a thing. Clothes are taken away, and with them the wallet or purse that contains driver's license, pictures of family, credit cards, all of the things we use daily to identify ourselves. We are given a gown that allows for no modesty and provides little warmth. Someone enters the room who may well be a stranger with a stethoscope around his (her) neck, looks at a chart, takes our pulse, pokes and prods, listens to lungs and heart, and says little. Someone else comes with a wheel chair, whisks us down the hall into an elevator, down several floors to an X-ray room where we have to wait while the technician finishes with the person on the table. When our turn finally arrives, we have to get up on the table, still dressed in that no-modesty gown, lie under that giant camera, and turn this way and that way and "hold your breath" and "don't move." So that by the time you get back into the room, and into bed, you are exhausted with no say in what is taking place. Thinghood!

A chaplain is the one person on the hospital staff who has no obvious reason to be in the patient's room. To enter that room, and enable relationship to happen is ministry. When a patient begins to talk about themselves, family, the work they do, that patient is moving away from thinghood back to personhood. If they mention the church to which they belong, a Sunday school class they teach, a Bible-study group, then the door is open to ask if they would like prayer. This is quite different from going into that room, and dumping prayer upon them whether they want it or not. No matter how pious sounding the words, the person in the bed can easily feel manipulated. That feeling is related to thinghood.

That wasn't taught to me in seminary. Nor does it come to a person just because they have been ordained. I recall that during those first weeks, when I was talking with a patient, I often tried to move the conversation around to baseball, or World War II. Those were topics about which I felt knowledgeable, thus comfortable. I was ministering to myself when that happened. The non-threatening help of the staff enabled me to look at myself in action. Growth and learning began to take place.

While telling of this, I must not leave an impression that all was work and no play. Anne and I had a fine relationship, a relationship in which we were both growing. While still in seminary she had given me a set of golf clubs on my birthday. Along the way we bought her a beginner's set of lady's clubs from Sears. Very early while in Winston-Salem we discovered Tanglewood Golf Course. Tanglewood was a beautiful 18-hole course designed by Robert Trent Jones, Jr. It was a public course. The greens fee was $3 for 18 h9oles, and at that time it was possible for a couple to buy an annual membership for $125. That membership allowed unlimited play. Autumn in North Carolina was beautiful that year. On my afternoon off I would meet Anne when she got off duty at the hospital, and we would drive the 16 miles out to Tanglewood, and play until it was too dark to see the ball. Obviously, we weren't able to complete 18 holes, but we didn't care. Golfers in that area didn't like to pay the $3 greens fee at that time of day since they couldn't complete the round. Consequently, there were times when Anne and I were alone on the course. That is the best $125 we ever spent. When we got back to the city, we then ate at the K and W Cafeteria. It was as good as the Psychologist at the hospital had said.

At the end of the six weeks of orientation, the interns began to do counseling. The staff secretary made the appointments. As you would guess, there was a central waiting area where the secretary had her desk. Counseling was done in private rooms, of course. Each room had a desk and two chairs. On the desk, unknown to the client, there was a microphone that enabled one of the staff to listen and record what took place. Later on, during one of our meetings, one of those counseling sessions could be the focus, part of the tape played, then discussion about what went on during the hour. In this way we learned to listen, really listen, to what that person was feeling. Dr. Young was our mentor. He had good insight into the psychological make-up of people, and the things that hurt, and can cripple one emotionally. He once said to us that it isn't some kind of esoteric skill or knowledge that the counselor dispenses to the patient that brings healing. When there is the kind of environment in which the client feels understood, accepted, safe and able to talk about anything with no fear of being judged, then healing can happen. Something else Dr. Young said to us has stuck with me through the years, "If anyone ever lets you inside of their life, take off your shoes, that is holy ground." Slowly, sometimes painfully, I began to learn how to hear what the other person was trying to say.

So it was that the days and weeks went by. Visiting patients, writing verbatims, counseling, staff meetings, reading, conducting chapel services, and some golf. Now and then, something happened that was golden. The rooms in the hospital were semi-private. There were two persons to a room, each room with a bath. One day I was calling upon a new patient on my wing. Mrs. Peterson was an older lady with Sweden in her words. She was seated on the side of her bed, looking tired. As soon as she spoke I was reminded of Mrs. Magnusson, from out of my childhood years. After the Magnussons moved across the river, now and then mom and I walked over in the afternoon to visit. Mrs. Magnusson understood this small boy. While she had coffee and my mother had tea, she gave me a skorpa, a hard Swedish roll that I enjoyed immensely. During that first visit with Mrs. Peterson, I told her of Mrs. Magnusson and my enjoyment of skorpas. As the days went by during my visits with Mrs. Peterson, it became clear that she was in the hospital for the last time. Her daughter, who chanced to be there when I stopped by one day, said the doctor had told the family that her mother's heart was just worn out, and nothing could be done to change that. A morning or two after that, when I entered Mrs. Peterson's room, her eyes were closed. I quietly went and sat in the chair by her bed. She was breathing slowly, and occasionally moaning softly. After a while she opened her eyes, looked at me and said, "I am so tired." During earlier visits my prayers with her had been for healing, and being able to return to home and family. But now I asked,

"Would you like for me to pray, and say that you are tired, and that you would like for God to allow you to come to Him, and find rest?"

"Oh, yes please," she responded, and closed her eyes. I prayed that prayer. When I finished, Mrs. Peterson still kept her eyes closed for several moments. Then she looked at me, and said,

"I'll never forget you! I will look for you and find you, and I will make you some Swedish food." That was the last conversation that we had. I continue in the hope that she finds me.

The holiday season came and went. We were well into the hospital routine now. For the most part the medical staff accepted us, and even expressed positive things about our work with patients. The medial interns referred to us as, "The God Squad".

I found fulfillment in what I was doing. It may be that the years in the Navy made it so, but however, it happened, I function well in a structured environment. Before the year was completed, I knew that I wanted to continue my ministry as a hospital chaplain. All along the way, Anne was very supportive of me. Spring came and went, then summer. I chose several hospitals and wrote to the administrators about the possibility of a chaplain being added to their staff. You may well wonder why when I tell you the contacts were made with hospitals on the coast. The year in Missouri had brought home to both of us, that we didn't like living very far from the ocean. Weeks went by, and no door opened to me for continuing in a hospital chaplaincy. As the time to leave Winston-Salem drew near, Dr. Young, during a staff meeting one day, told us that he had been chosen to head a new ministry to the poor in Winston-Salem. He added that things were only at the planning stage, but he could foresee hiring some of the interns for that ministry. He added that he was very excited about what was happening. Just as in the Navy, there was scuttlebutt among the interns. Word got around that the pay for those hired by Dr. Young was to be $4,800 annually to begin. Frankly, at that time $4,800 seemed like quite a bit of money. The interns who were Baptists, received a stipend during the year of training. The three of us from other denominations, were not eligible for that remuneration, understandably so. That was a Baptist hospital, supported by Baptist people. Anne and I lived on her salary of $3,720 a year. So you can see that an income of $4,800 was not without appeal. I do not remember now how many interns Dr. Young needed for the project. When he interviewed me, I had to say that I wasn't eligible for several reasons. I wasn't ordained, I was responsible to San Francisco Presbytery, and in order to be ordained it was necessary to receive a call that met the approval of the Presbytery.

I don't know of anybody who likes "good byes". When the time comes to say goodbye to people about whom I have learned to care, I handle it in a stoic way, while feeling disgruntled inside. There was a graduation ceremony held in the hospital chapel. Each of the interns received a certificate on the completion of clinical-pastoral training. What that year meant to me personally, no certificate could reflect. Undoubtedly, it was one of the most important single years in my life, a year in which I learned much that enhanced my ministry, a year in which I learned much about myself as a person and why I functioned as I did. For instance, it came as revelation to me that if I did the opposite of what I thought my mother would want me to do, I was being controlled by her just as surely as if I did exactly what she wanted me to do. At the age of 37, I learned that if someone was angry with me, it didn't follow that they wanted to kill me. For all those years, if someone was expressing anger towards me, I felt as frightened as I had in the lagoon at Tarawa. As you well know, a reaction like that doesn't change in an easy way just because we understand what is happening. Understanding, however, opens the door for growth. Thanks, Dr. Young, and Herb Zerof, and Ben Patrick wherever you are.

Anne and I helped some of the other interns with their moving. Since we didn't have a call, or any prospects of one, we decided to head for Seattle to visit with Anne's family, and take in the last weeks of the World's Fair being held in that city. Bill and Gladys said we would be welcome to stay with them. So, not wanting to haul a trailer across country, we gave away everything that wouldn't fit in our car, and headed west.

There isn't much of note to say about the trip to Seattle. We have driven across country eight times, and across Canada once, and it becomes kind of a blue in my memory. However, this time we had the luxury of a pup tent we got with green stamps in Winston Salem. Previously we had slept in sleeping bags out in the open. Somewhere I heard or read of someone saying that their pup tent was so small they had to get outside to change their mind. For us that night at the campground in Tennessee, and through the other nights on that trip, it was luxury to have the privacy the tent afforded.

We stopped in Minnesota to visit Jay and Marilyn Curry. They had been good friends while sharing the intern experience. In Spokane we spent the night with Bob and Marilyn Gray, friends from the college and seminary years. Bob was assistant pastor at the Whitworth Presbyterian Church, working with students on campus.

Anne's brother, Bill, and his wife Gladys made us feel very welcome when we arrived at their place in Seattle. Bill was assistant pastor at Woodland Park Presbyterian Church, and enthused about his work. He took me to meet Neil Kuyper, who had organized a counseling service sponsored by Seattle Presbytery. He thought that if there was any inclination by Neil to begin expanding the Counseling Service, with my clinical pastoral training, maybe something would work out. The visit with Neil was interesting. During that conversation, Neil mentioned that he could use some help, but at that point it would only be on a part time basis. He wondered if I would be interested, if it could be worked out. It would mean working two days weekly at the Counseling Service, and the rest of the time as assistant pastor for one of the local churches. It looked to me as though there was little likelihood of me becoming a hospital chaplain. Working even part time as a counselor would utilize some of the skills I had acquired during the year at the hospital. I told Neil that I was interested.

Anne and I spent a couple of days attending the World's Fair. It would have taken much more time than that to see all there was to see. We rode the Monorail, and went up to the top of the Space Needle, and looked at as many exhibits as we could in the time we allotted for the purpose. Both Bill and Neil had let me know that work had begun on seeing if the Presbytery would be willing to add to the staff of the Counseling Service, adding that those things take time. Bill and Gladys had two preschool children, and we didn't want to overstay our welcome. It had been two years since seeing our Walnut Creek friends. Our good friend Ida was recovering from hip surgery so we made arrangements to stay with her. Visiting with Ida was like a visit home. Walnut Creek has a special place in my life, and in our marriage. Ray and Lu Brooks are like family.

Bob Kellog, at whose gymnasium I had been a member for two summers during the Whitworth years, had opened a restaurant where the gym had been. When I stopped by to say hello, he offered me a job as dishwasher until something opened up in the church. I was grateful.

Did I mention earlier that Ray Brooks and I had occasionally talked about our different Navy experience, he as a PBY pilot, and I as a signalman on a Destroyer? One evening after I finished my shift washing dishes, I received a telephone call from Ray. With surprise in his voice, he said,

"Hey Souce, listen to what I just read in the Walnut Kernal." The Walnut Kernal was the local newspaper that came out once a week. Ray then went on to read to me an obituary notice, telling of the death of Rear Admiral Thomas F. Conley, Jr. In the obituary, it mentioned that as a young Captain of the Ringgold he had taken his ship into the lagoon at Tarawa. Ray remembered me having been on the Ringgold, and that the Captain's name had been Conley.

What Ray had just told me staggered my credulity. I got Ida's copy of the Walnut Kernal, and read the obituary notice for myself. Since retiring from the Navy, Admiral Conley had been teaching at Oakland City College. He and his wife had been living in Walnut Creek for the last five years. The notice went on to say that there was to be a Rosary held at Hull's Funeral Home the next evening at 8 PM, and a 9 AM mass the next morning at St. Mary's Catholic Church. My mind was unable to embrace in any logical way any of this. When I reported aboard the Ringgold, Collinsville, Connecticut was my home. Captain Conley's home was Bridgeport, Connecticut. Now, twenty years later, we were in the same California town, and Captain Conley had died. He and his wife had moved there the year I graduated from Whitworth. That summer I had lived with Ida while working at the oil refinery. The next summer after my first year of seminary, Anne and I married and spent the summer living in Ida's house while she worked at a church conference center. I worked at the oil refinery again, and Anne worked as a nurse at the local Kaiser hospital. How many times during those two summers did I come close to crossing paths with Captain Conley? I would have so much enjoyed meeting and talking with him. Would he have remembered, the phone talker he often addressed, "Soucy Goddamit"? I was grieving, but unable to give myself permission to weep. The next evening as I got ready to go to the Funeral Home, Anne asked if I wanted her to come with me. I told her it was something I had to do alone. When I arrived at Hull's, the attendant greeted me at the door, and had me sign the Guest Book. When I entered the chapel, nobody else was there. I walked to the front where the open casket was. Admiral Conley, was in his dress blues, his Admiral's hat resting on a three legged stool close by. He didn't look much different than he had on the Ringgold. Many thoughts raced through my mind, and it occurred to me as I stood there, that I was the same age, 38 years old, that he had been when we put the Ringgold in commission. The organist, unseen, began to play traditional funeral type music, so I went and sat down on the left side of the chapel. Several people had come in and were sitting on the other side. Just before the priest came out, the organist swung into *Anchors Away*. Then I cried! I wept as I hadn't wept for years.

After the service, the few others present, members of the family I guess, filed past the casket. I went out and got into my car. Still weeping, I drove around Walnut Creek. I suspect that many years of unshed tears were flowing that night. After a while I stopped at the Brooks' home. Ray was someone who would understand, and one of few people I didn't mind seeing me with red eyes. I don't know what we talked about that night, or what time I went home to Anne and Ida. The next morning, Anne and I went to where the Roman Catholic Church has their building on Mt. Diablo Blvd. for the Funeral Mass. Unlike the Rosary service the night before, the Church building was packed. I knew that the Mass would have been very important to Thomas F. Conley, Jr. However, my feeling was that we should be on a Destroyer at sea, and after the service, sewed up in canvas with two five inch shells for weight, the body dropped to the sea below. Captain Conley was a sailor. I am proud to have served under his command.

A few days later, after calling first, Anne and I visited with his widow at their home on Van Cleve Lane. If there is such a thing as a typical Navy wife, that's how Kathryn Conley struck me. On the mantle over the fireplace there was a model of the Ringgold. It was a good visit.

Around the middle of December I received word that Seattle Presbytery had approved hiring a part time counselor to work with Neal, and that we needed to return to Washington. The next weeks were busy. In a very short period, I was approved by the Counseling Service Oversight Committee from Presbytery for Tuesdays and Wednesdays, and called by the Lake Forest Park Presbyterian Church to be assistant pastor Thursday through Sunday. Monday was to be my day off. My salary was $4,800, with a housing allowance of $1,200. After the $250 monthly salary for the 13 months in Mound City, and living on Anne's salary as a nurse for the past two years, we both felt wealthy. One other item here, I was examined by the Ministerial Relations Committee to determine if I was suitable for ordination. Then I had to appear before the whole Presbytery. The service of ordination took place at the Lake Forest Park church in April. Several things need to be mentioned here. One of them is that I should not have taken a job with an emphasis upon Christian Education. I didn't know that. Many of my classmates at Princeton had done exactly that same thing. It was a common practice. I was not qualified to be a Minister of Christian Education. During the three years of seminary I had one course having to do with that discipline. At that time there were students at seminary, female usually, who spent three years acquiring a Master's Degree in Religious Education. That was the kind of person that Lake Forest Park needed, but they got me. I wonder how many Seminary graduates at that time were making the same mistake? My call had other built in problems, because of the split nature of the call.

The Counseling Service had me for two days each week, they were not to contact me at any other time. Lake Forest Park had me Thursday through Sunday, they were not to call upon me on other days. It didn't work that way. I had two bosses. The wrinkles in my personality make-up are such that I have difficulty when there is just one.

As soon as we were settled we began the process of adopting a child. Needless to say that it wasn't simple. In addition it became necessary to get a loan to pay the expenses involved. March 6, 1964 Glenn was born, weighing 10 pounds, 6 ½ ounces. Six days later we brought home our son. I well remember the sense of joy and pride when we stopped on the way home and introduced him to Bill and Gladys. Glenn David Soucy was a welcome addition to our family, and he added joy to our life together.

Toward the end of the second year of my split ministry, I was informed that the Counseling Service was going to increase my position to full time. A committee was formed by Presbytery to deal with this. Understandably so, I was considered to be a candidate. The Presbytery Executive talked with me about that, and said that I could have the position if I wanted it. At that point, I fully intended to apply. However, after an unpleasant confrontation with Neil that had to do with me not reporting to him in a way he thought I should, I decided to withdraw my name from consideration for the full time position. I wrote a letter to that effect to the committee. After Neil heard of that, he came to me in my office saying that my action kind of shook him up. Then he added, "I guess you know that you have an authority problem." On one of those rare occasions when the mind works fast enough, I responded. "Sure, we both do Neil. You have to be one, and I can't handle that." Thus ended my split ministry.

I wound up my work at the Counseling Service the end of December. Fortunately for us, Lake Forest Park church kept me on until I received a call from a small congregation in Onalaska,

Washington. It was during the last few weeks in Seattle that a baby girl was born. On April 16th 1965, we adopted our second child, Karen Anne.

Onalaska is two hours south of Seattle, five miles east of Interstate 5. It is a small town, once the home of the largest lumber mill on the West Coast. The owner closed the mill during WW II because of a labor dispute. When we moved there, the village had a school, two small grocery stores, a barber shop, a tavern, two gas stations, an oil distributor, a small one man lumber mill, and three churches. The Community Presbyterian Church Building had been built at the beginning of WWI. According to the story told me, the owner of the mill went to his employees asking for donations, and donated the rest himself. The manse, built at the same time, had seven rooms, and a small one-car garage, a dandy house for the four of us. Oh, I mustn't forget our dog, Tiger. He liked living there, too.

I was 40, and Anne 33 when we made that move, Glenn was almost 14 months old, Karen was two weeks. Need I say that Anne had her hands full? So did I! Small town ministry is unique. The thirteen months spent in Mound City provided an excellent apprenticeship. We were there for almost five years.

What can I say about those years? I'd like to recount tales of miracles taking place, and of persons dramatically changed. I guess the real miracle is that those people put up with me that long. We did the things of life just as you did. The Plymouth wore out. We bought our first new vehicle, a Chevrolet pick-up. Then we bought a used 16' trailer that we pulled with the pick-up for family vacations at the ocean. I conducted worship services, married people, buried others, baptized a few. The kids grew, and hopefully so did we.

November 1969, my mother came for a visit. We exchanged weekly letters, but we hadn't seen her since graduation from seminary, eight years previously. While she was there, I received a telephone call from the chairman of a pastor seeking committee for the Presbyterian Church at South Lake Tahoe, California. They had reviewed my dossier and wanted to hear me preach and interview me. It was arranged that I catch a flight down to Reno, preach at St. John's Presbyterian Church, then meet with the pastor seeking committee that afternoon, and fly back home the next day. Mom had to leave while I was gone. She was scheduled to fly to Texas to visit with my brother Brian. It had been a good visit with her. The best ever! Maybe I was growing up just a little bit? The flight to Reno was routine. I went down on Saturday, checked in with the pastor, Bill Clausen, so that he would know I had arrived. Also, that gave me the opportunity to get a feel for the sanctuary, rather than just walk in there cold on Sunday morning before preaching. Since it was November, the time of the year when most congregations were dealing with next year's budget, the topic of my sermon was stewardship. I hope that what I did that morning was worthwhile for those present. Whether it turned out that way or not, only someone who was there that morning could say.

I do not recall if there was one or two services that morning at St. John's. There were five members of the pastor seeking committee who introduced themselves to me after I was through. Their faces are in my memory as though it was just a day or two ago: Evelyn Grau, Roberta Mason, Harry Wadman, Jerry Johnson, and Bruce Cook. Bruce was chairman, and it had been he who had talked with me over the telephone. We drove to South Lake Tahoe, and they took me to the church building. Chairs were set in a circle in a room off the sanctuary, which they called the Fireside Room. As you would readily guess, the room had a fireplace, also a sink with cupboards, a natural place for people to stop after Sunday Services, and talk together while having a cup of tea or coffee. I do not recall much about the interview with that committee. I do know that I was impressed with what that congregation had done with their place of worship. After the members of the committee were through with any questions they had, we went to Evelyn Grau's home for a buffet dinner. Her husband, John had everything ready when we arrived. For reasons unclear to me, I really do not enjoy eating a meal with a group of people I do not know. Well, that is not the total picture. I really do not enjoy eating with large groups of people, whether I know them or not. Maybe that is a carry over from those Navy years, and so many meals eaten in mess halls. In any case, I think that I have successfully dealt with that feeling through the years without making the people around me uncomfortable.

It was a very friendly atmosphere that afternoon. John Grau had done a good job with that buffet meal of roast turkey, and all of the trimmings. When we finished, Bruce and Jerry gave me a ride back to my motel in Reno. I had no clue what the committee's thinking was, except for Harry Wadman. Harry and his wife owned a music store not far from where the church building was located on the main thoroughfare, which passes through South Lake Tahoe on the way to Nevada. Harry appeared to be around 60 years old, he sounded a bit gruff when he spoke. During the meeting with the committee in the Fireside Room, Harry had said that after the sermon he didn't need to ask me any questions. He didn't expand on that, but my impression was that he approved of what he had heard.

When I got to the Portland Airport, it was joy to see Anne and the kids. Naturally, Anne was curious. I told her what had taken place, and my positive impressions of people I met, and of the church building. Late that afternoon I received a telephone call from Bruce Cook, the committee had met and were recommending me to the congregation. The next step was to arrange a Sunday when I could lead the congregation in worship, following which there would be a vote on whether to call me as pastor. When the conversation was over, with a sense of joy I told Anne.

The Onalaska congregation was in the midst of it's own stewardship campaign. I felt it important not to disrupt that. It was not yet Christmas when I went down to be presented to the congregation in California. They voted to issue a call to me. Bruce asked when I would be able to begin. Just prior to Christmas seemed to me as though it would be a poor time to tell the Onalaska congregation that we would be leaving, so I made arrangements to begin my work at South Lake Tahoe on the first Sunday in February.

It is a customary practice for the calling church to pay the moving expenses of a pastor. Anne did most of the packing during those last few weeks we were in Onalaska. We made arrangements with a Moving Company to haul our belongings. Maybe it says more about us than it does the congregation, but we never really felt at home during that five years we were there. Only a few people ever reached out to us as friends. Anne by nature is far more a social person than I am. To be sure, much of her energy and time was invested in our two preschool children, but only one woman treated her as a friend during those years. To be sure, those women has their own responsibilities and every day concerns. Anyway, maybe you understand when I say that we were glad to be leaving. I don't think I am exaggerating when I express the guess that there was probably some there who shared the feeling. The moving van picked up our furniture. We hooked the pickup to the trailer and headed south. Something else going on in me was the feeling that in returning to Northern California, I was coming home. If I am going to feel down, it is more likely to happen on a rainy day. During the seven years we spent in Western Washington, there were a large number of rainy days, so by the time we left my spirit was wrinkled like a washerwoman's finger tips. The anticipation of being pastor at South Lake Tahoe was warm inside me.

In order to avoid traveling over Echo Summit, whish is over 7,000 feet elevation, we drove through Susanville, and up to South Lake Tahoe from the east. It was evening when we got to lake level, and it just started to snow lightly. We were fortunate! What a pleasure to drive into the parking lot where the manse is. I guess I hadn't mentioned that the manse was part of the church building. Originally they had been separate structures adjacent to each other. Under the ministry of Irv Morris, who preceded me as pastor, the congregation had undertaken a renovation program in which a magnificent job had been done. Now the manse, and church building are one structure and very pleasing to the eye.

Make no mistake about it, there are disadvantages in living that close to the church building. If some group needs the heat turned on, guess who they call to do it. If someone walking or driving by needs help you know whose doorbell is rung. On the other hand, living in snow country, it is very convenient not to have to travel to get to work.

Harry Wadman, at his music store just a couple of blocks from us, had the key to the manse. He came over to let us in, and welcome us. If you have been around small children it won't be difficult for you to picture the excitement of our two. Glenn was five years old, and Karen four. I had been through the manse during my other visits, but this was all new to Anne and the kids. While Anne was admiring the kitchen, Glenn and Karen ran upstairs to see the bedrooms. Glenn immediately chose the first one, which he thought was best. Karen gladly took the other one which had a grand view across a big meadow and out to the lake. The upstairs had its own bathroom. The Moving Van with our furniture wasn't due until the next day, but we had sleeping bags and blankets. The process of getting settled in a new home has its problems, but we managed with very little stress as I recall. Anne is very proficient at such things.

One of the first things we had to face was getting Glenn enrolled in Kindergarten. He made the change very well. My new office was located just across the hall from the kitchen, and it was easy to begin work. Someone had planned a congregational potluck supper and entertainment as a welcoming program for us our first Saturday evening in town. House warming gifts were presented to us. The wife of the editor of the local newspaper told me on the side that she wanted to bring a bottle of scotch but didn't know if she could get away with it. So we began what turned out to be almost 11 years as pastor of the Presbyterian Church at South Lake Tahoe, California. February 1970—December 1980, the happiest years of my ministry.

South Lake Tahoe is an unusual city. The eastern border ends at Stateline, Nevada, a gambling center with four beautiful casinos. On one side is that beautiful lake, and on the other the Sierras, with ski resorts easily seen from the highway going through the center of town. Needless to add, perhaps, tourism is a major source of income. As a consequence, the city population is quite transient, and that is carried over into the church's life. Many of the congregations in town were having difficulty. During our first year there, both the Methodist and Episcopalian congregations decided to shut down. A few families from each of those small congregations decided to worship with us. We were the richer for their presence, but the Presbyterians weren't exactly thriving. When I began, the church was encumbered by two bank loans that made a large demand upon the monthly income. The money from these loans had been for the building program. So, as with others in the city, the Presbyterian congregation had its problems, but there was a good spirit in those who were there.

It would have been easy to supplement our family income by having a marriage business during those years. From the very beginning there were many telephone calls, or couples just dropping by, inquiring about having a wedding. This was quite different from the way it had been in Onalaska. Because of that difference, wanting to have an idea of how many requests were received, I began keeping track on my calendar. During the first 11 months I received 86 requests from couples wishing to be married at South Lake Tahoe.

When I was ordained I decided that I wouldn't accept money for taking part in weddings or funerals. This was a personal decision. There were no guidelines. It was my understanding that the congregation paid a pastor's salary in order to free him (her) to provide ministry to the community. So it seemed inappropriate for me to accept money for what I was already getting paid to do. That decision made, there was no thought of becoming a "Marrying Sam" in order to make money on the side. I also knew that I didn't care to have the Presbyterian Church building being used as a Wedding Chapel like those available just down the road on the Nevada side of the state line. Given the luxury of looking back, I wish that from the beginning I had refused to take part in a wedding unless the people were related to the congregation for which I was pastor. However, I didn't have that luxury, and I began by telling people they would have to meet with me for three one hour sessions prior to the wedding ceremony if they wanted me to conduct the ceremony. That cut down considerably on the number of weddings that took place with me as minister. Even so I had more than 20 weddings that first year, far too many for the pastor of a small congregation.

During the three sessions with a couple, I talked with them about how to manage money, the sexual relationship, and fighting fair. My impression is that most, if not all, of those couples put up with that because it was required if they wished to be married in South Lake Tahoe at the Presbyterian Church building. During those eleven years, one couple stopped by a year after the ceremony thanking me for the instruction on how to manage their money. Aside from that,

I don't recall ever seeing, or hearing, from any couple from out of town whose wedding ceremony I preformed. After a few years, I decided not to take part in a wedding unless the people were part of the congregation. Needless to say perhaps, now and then I was on the receiving end of some rather 'barbed' comments from a caller wishing to be married there, and learning that it wasn't possible. For a fellow who couldn't handle disapproval for many years, I had come a long way.

In the way it is with life, the months and years went by. New people joined the congregation, others moved away, and some just dropped out, but there was a strong permanent group with whom it was a pleasure to serve. I was blessed with a good worship committee: Bill Fairley, a school counselor, who was also choir director for the church, Vivian Tisher, a school teacher, Elaine Hawkins married to a casino worker, Marie Cluiff, a school teacher and married to a teacher. We met once a week. Very early in our work together we tried to ask ourselves, "If I wished to worship God, how would I do that?" This led to a great deal of soul searching and study in the recognition that something doesn't become worship just because we give it that name. To serve God with worship! How do we do that? I remember Vivian saying

"Since it is to be an offering by a congregation it can't be a spectator event." We dealt with what it means that there is to be an order of worship, not something that just happens in an automatic way, but rather something that is planned. Order presupposes an underlying principle out of which the order comes. (My eternal gratitude to Dr. Donald MaCleod, Professor of Worship at Princeton.) We each felt, when we thought about it, that we were well versed in being casual. We needed the church to nurture us in reverence. The committee developed an order of worship that was an ascending order of vision and response, with reverence for God at the heart of what we were trying to do.

The governing body of the church, the Session, was very supportive of its committees. They didn't automatically approve all recommendations, but they did take seriously the work a committee had done. When the Worship Committee recommended changes in the order of worship, with explanation of what we were trying to have happen, the Session approved.

Taking their task seriously, the members of the committee knew better than to begin the new worship service without informing people of the congregation. The next few weeks had a member of the committee at both worship services telling those present what was going to be different. The most obvious change, and one most likely to meet with resistance, had to do with the Offering part of worship. Traditionally, this had been ushers passing plates in which people placed their offering. The committee's thinking was that this was too much like taking up a collection, an unpleasant bit of business, rather than an act of reverent worship. In the ascending order of vision and response, the Proclamation (sermon) was intended to be the highest act of vision, and the Offering immediately following, the highest act of response. It was decided that this was most likely to happen if people brought their offering personally and put it in a receptacle placed on the altar in front of the Communion Table. People were asked to bring their offering forward using the center aisle, and returning to their seats using the side aisles. It is gratifying the way the people of that congregation responded. While they were offering their gifts, the choir sang:

> *"Thanks be to God, the Father Almighty,*
> *Thanks be to God, who came to this earth.*
> *Thanks be to God, the Spirit Eternal.*
> *Thanks be to God forever!"*

As the people of the congregation got used to the new way of presenting their offering as a conscious act of worship, they were encouraged to sing along with the choir. Most of them did. As far as I know, nobody ever complained about the change.

Someone may well wonder about Proclamation as the highest expression of vision. That places a great burden upon the preacher. However, it seem to me that burden is already there by implication. Up to one-third of the time a congregation allocates for worship is spent upon the sermon. Did I meet that awesome responsibility as a preacher? The only honest answer is that I don't know. Very early in my experience as part of the church, I came to some conclusions about preaching:

> Good preaching is rare.
>
> It doesn't draw attention to itself.
>
> It appears to be easy to do.
>
> It is never boring.
>
> It leaves the hearer wishing it wasn't over.

Consequently, by the time I got to seminary I had a personal commitment to work at not being a bore. During the thirteen months in Mound City, I had developed a system for sermon preparation that worked for me. Part of that preparation was a decision made at seminary not to use notes. That meant I had to work with what I intended to say until it was part of me. Not unlike an actor getting ready to take part in a stage play. To be truthful, I saw myself as an actor in the drama of worship. Every Sunday during all those years, when it was time for me to enter the sanctuary and lead in worship, I had the feeling that I had something worth saying. I suspect that not every person who was present would agree, but at least I was trying.

Each pastor in the denomination is provided with two weeks of study leave annually. This can be carried over for a maximum of six years so that one is able to have three months for an extended period of study. I allowed mine to accumulate, because there was nothing that had any appeal to me. Nothing, that is, until I read an article in which Henri Nouwen was being interviewed. Henri Nouwen was a Roman Catholic priest, teaching at Yale Divinity School. At the time of the interview Nouwen was preparing to take a six-month sabbatical to spend at a Trappist monastery. The article was centered in wondering why a man teaching pastoral care to budding Protestant ministers would feel the need to spend time in solitude at a monastery. What Henri Nouwen said in that interview struck a chord deep within me. There is a long tradition of silence and prayer about which I knew next to nothing. I felt a deep down hunger to spend my three months of study leave in a monastery. Whether or not this was even possible, I had no idea.

I wrote to Henri Nouwen at Yale Divinity School early autumn, 1974. His reply arrived in October, It had been written from the monastery where he was taking his sabbatical. In his letter he encouraged me to pursue my desire to spend my study leave with a contemplative community. He suggested two possibilities" Mount Savior Monastery outside of Elmira, N. Y., and a university run by Benedictine monks at Collegeville, Minnesota. Immediately, I knew that Mount Savior was what I was seeking. Fr. Nouwen gave me the name of Brother Peter, Guest Master, and the address of the monastery. My nature is such, that when I am planning something, I desire having confirmation right now, or even sooner. From the very beginning I had been talking with Anne about what I was feeling. She read the interview that had piqued my interest, and of course I showed her my letters, and the answers when they arrived. At this stage it was all rather nebulous. I wrote to Brother Peter, telling him what I was thinking. His reply came in the middle of November. He was encouraging, but indicated that it wasn't by any means certain that they could receive me. Thus began a long process in which I was trying to obtain permission to spend three months at Mount Savior during the summer of 1976.

I needed the permission of my family. I broached the subject one evening while we were eating dinner. Glenn was almost 11 and Karen a year younger. Anne has always supported me in the things I felt I needed to do. I already knew that she was willing to deal with what it would mean for me to be gone for three months. After I spoke of what I had in mind, Glenn immediately said that it was fine with him. Karen looked at me and asked,

"Does it make any difference what I think?" I assured her that it did. She said, "I want to think about it for awhile, before I decide." I told her that would be fine even though inside I wanted to have that hurdle out of the way. Just before Christmas at dinner one evening, Karen said,

"I don't think I am going to like it, but you have my permission to be gone for three months."

Then began the long wait until I heard one way or another from the monastic community. It was 1975, and my sabbatical wasn't until 1976. Caught up in the things of parish ministry, only occasionally was there a passing thought about the possibility that we would be separated for three months. Finally, in November, I received a short note from Fr. Martin saying that I would be received as a guest, and that May, June, and July would be good months in which I could help him with the garden. Suddenly the reality of our being apart for three months confronted us. I began the process of trying to get the necessary approval of my plans from the ecclesiastical hierarchy.

In January I received word from Dick Pearson, chairman of the Presbytery's "Minister and the Church" committee that my plans had been approved. All signs were go! Along the way, I informed the Session of what I was trying to do. I needed their approval, too. We began the process of trying to find an interim pastor during the period I would be absent. By way of the monthly newsletter, I explained, or tried to, my plans and hopes for the study leave to the people of the congregation.

Before I forget, Anne and I thought it would be nice to have a special family vacation prior to my being gone for three months. For many years we had been saving for a trip to Hawaii. When we walked each morning we picked up aluminum cans along the route. The money we got when we turned them in went into the Hawaii Fund. Since Glenn was to be twelve on his next birthday, we would then need to pay adult fare for his ticket, all the more reason to go before then. Looming even larger was the offered hospitality of friends living on the island of Kauai. Bill and Jan Shirley, with their four children, had moved to Kauai from South Lake Tahoe. They had been active church members, and good friends. Bill, a retired Naval aviator, and I played tennis together during their time at Tahoe. They knew about our Hawaii fund, and in one of their letters to us, they wondered about the possibility of exchanging houses with us sometime. They could get in some good skiing, and we could enjoy Kauai. Now we pursued that possibility with them for the end of December, and the first week in January. We proceeded with our plans with that in mind. It almost worked. To our dismay, as the time drew near, Bill called us to say that It just wouldn't work at their end to come to the lake at this time. However, he went on to assure me that they would be glad to have us during those two weeks. So that's what we did.

It would be difficult for me to exaggerate what a glorious two weeks that was. As we flew over Pearl Harbor on our way to the Honolulu airport I thought of the many times the Ringgold sailed in and out of that harbor. Much to our surprise a young lady met us and placed a lei around each of our necks, as we were on the way to catch the shuttle plane to Kauai, a gift of welcome arranged by the Board of Deacons back at Tahoe. All of the Shirleys were waiting for us at the airport on Kauai. It was joy to see them again. They had arranged with their good neighbors, Guy and Lynn Nunn, for us to use their guest cottage for sleeping. The Shirley's were delightful hosts. We swam at Poipu beach most days. They suggested that we leave Glenn and Karen with them while we took a couple of days to explore the island. What we saw reminded me of the way things had been when I was growing up in Collinsville, life lived at a slower pace. At the time there were just two traffic lights on the whole island. When we returned to the Shirleys, there was an invitation to dinner from a local doctor. Mary Thompson, who was a member of the church at Tahoe, had been raised on Kauai. It was her brother who gave us the invitation. My memories of that evening have dimmed considerably, but strong is the memory of that nice family, and their warm hospitality. Mary arranged another wonderful gift. When we returned to the airport, another brother met us with a box of pineapple to take back home. As we sat on the airplane waiting for take off, looking out the window at the Shirley family waving good bye, we both were choked with tears. How I wish that I could have given myself permission to weep. That's what I needed to do.

When we got back home it seemed as though there was little time before I was to leave for the monastery. It had been fifteen years since last I had seen my family in Connecticut, and it made good sense to visit. My brother Denis had agreed to meet me at the airport, and after several days visit with my mom and Fred, he was to drive me to the monastery.

The weeks before I left went too fast. When Anne and the kids took me to the airport in Reno, the lump in my throat had me wondering why I was doing this. Here again, another of those times when I was saying "good-bye" to those I'd much rather be saying "hello" to. The three months of separation is high on the list of most difficult things done in my life. Nevertheless, I am glad that we did it.

The time spent at MT. Savior is a whole tale in itself. I went there seeking silence, thinking that in the silent place something special would happen. What I learned was, if there is rioting on the streets of one's soul, what silence does, is reveal that. I wonder if that is why we fill our lives with noise? Can it be that we dread facing ourselves in the silence? When there is quietness within, there is no need to hide in back of words, or television, or whatever. Something else I learned from the monks, and this is no small thing, they nurtured me in the reverent worship of God. This they did, not by talking about it, but by example. When we were serving God with our offering of worship, reverence was in the air that we breathed. That has not been as evident in my experience of many Protestant Sunday services.

Dr. Buttrick once said in class, "We've made following Jesus, like 'going to church'." In that observation there is painful truth. We are raised in a culture that teaches us to think of ourselves as people who 'go to church', or who don't go or who go sometimes. As a consequence, the church becomes a building, a place with an address, a place that one can go to, and then leave. That is contrary to what the New Testament reveals. In Jesus' thinking the church was people, never a place. He invited persons to follow him, those who accepted the invitation were "the called out ones", the church. This community, made up of his followers, has a life to live in response to God. One expression of that life lived in response, is to serve God with our offering of worship. If it is your intent to serve God with worship, have you spent time and thought on how to do that? Clearly something doesn't become worship just because we give it that name, or because we do it in a particular building. Any worship worthy to be called that, must be centered in God rather than ourselves, something we do, rather than something to be received, rooted in reverence, never casual or frivolous. Not that many years ago, I was attending a Sunday service, seated toward the front as people were entering the sanctuary. It was very noisy! The thought came to me, "If these folks were gathering for a barn dance, the only difference would be the smell of hay in the air."

My spirit hungers for the service of worship offered at Mt. Savior. Each Sunday morning people from the surrounding area came to the monastery. They began arriving early, so it became my practice to be in the chapel by 8:45. Something in me likes to sit in the same place each week. The chapel was for offering worship. It was erected and furnished for that purpose, a holy place! Roman Catholics understand that. They enter quietly, bow towards the altar before sitting down, no talking. Seated there in the quiet, a person has opportunity to think, prepare for worship. It may well be different for you, but I am not naturally a reverent person. My nature is to be casual, irreverent. My crying need is for the church to nourish me in reverence. That's what happened at Mt. Savior. I am indebted to those monks. I went to them as a stranger, they received me as a guest, and finally made me feel at home. Well, not exactly at home, but you know what I mean.

My home was with Anne, Glenn, and Karen. I had no idea how difficult it would be to be away from them for that period of time. When the last day of July arrived, waiting for Anne to come and get me was like waiting for Christmas when I was a child. The transition from life at the monastery, back to life as a parish minister at South Lake Tahoe went smoothly. I was home! Time went by rapidly, or so it seems in memory.

When I had been there for ten years, I began to pick up signals that indicated to me that it was time for me to leave. This was no sudden impression, but something that grew over a period of a year. Bob Graham was the Mission Area Executive. I talked with him about what I was feeling, and he agreed that after ten years the congregation and I could both benefit from a change. In one of our conversations I mentioned to him that I would be interested in doing interim ministry. At that time in the life of the national church, interim ministry was something done mainly by retired pastors. It had been the custom through the years, when a congregation was between pastors, to have a retired pastor come for things like leading in worship. However, it had gotten to be usual for pastor seeking committees to spend about a year in their search for a new pastor. That is a long period for a congregation to be without a minister in residence. So the practice had grown for congregations to invite someone to be pastor during the interim period. It was to that kind of interim ministry that I felt drawn as a challenging and interesting way to spend the next years of my active ministry. Little did I know! In my mind's eye, was the picture of a congregation having had a pastor for a number of years, the pastor retiring or leaving for a new charge, a natural sense of loss being felt by the people. I would be there during the interim period, providing pastoral care, helping them deal with their grief, preparing the way for their new pastor. It didn't happen quite that way.

Of course, Anne and I were in conversation about all of this during many months. Glenn and Karen were in high school, and we didn't care to add worry to their days, so it didn't come up with them until there was something definite about leaving South Lake Tahoe. It wouldn't have been fair to expect our children to move around every year while I was doing interim pastorates. We agreed that what made most sense was to move to a place we were buying for future retirement as our permanent residence. While serving a congregation as interim, I would have to be away during the week, home on my days off. The three months spent in the monastery, as difficult as being apart was, had helped us know how to handle that. It's a good thing it did. My first invitation to be interim was for a congregation more than 200 miles from home. My thoughts of helping a congregation grieve over the loss of a loved pastor didn't apply. This congregation had fired their pastor. That was something, in my experience, almost unheard of in the life of the church.

It was understandably difficult to leave South Lake Tahoe. Oh, I don't mean the city. I mean the people of that congregation. We had been there almost eleven years, and made many friends. That was a lot of growing up time for our children. They complained about having to make the move. Something that made the transition easier for me was Al and Mary Lu Suneson. They were members of the congregation in Madera where I was going. Al had been chairman of the committee that chose me as interim pastor. He wrote a letter expressing pleasure that I was to be their pastor for the coming months. In addition he invited me to stay with them until I found an apartment. He said that they both enjoyed company, and I didn't need to have a sense of urgency about finding a place. That felt good. It took a great deal of pressure off of me. How very thoughtful of the Sunesons!

The last Sunday of November 1980 was the end of my ministry at South Lake Tahoe. The Session gave permission for Anne, Glenn, and Karen to stay in the manse until the semester was over at the high school. I headed for Madera, planning to get established there, and to return home on Christmas Eve. There is little need to tell of things like finding an apartment, moving the family to Slug Gulch Road, or how boring were those three hour trips between Madera and home. Within three weeks, both Glenn and Karen told me how much they liked the high school in Placerville. That was a relief. How was interim ministry in Madera? Nothing like I thought it would be. At my first session meeting, one of the elders moved that the session take its responsibility seriously and sever the ties with the Presbyterian Church. Talk about, "Joy To The World". What a relief when the motion died for want of a second. What a wake up call to have me know I wasn't in for a fun year of just helping a congregation through a period of grief having lost a well loved pastor.

I was with those folks a little more than 17 months. The pastor seeking committee worked hard. They finally decided upon a young couple just graduating from San Anselmo Seminary. For good reasons, an interim minister has very little contact with the pastor seeking committee in it's work. However, after the call to that young couple was issued, three members of that committee individually, and at different times, told me of one of the candidates in his early thirties who they personally would have preferred for themselves, but they thought the young couple would be better for the congregation as a whole. That is selflessness. It spoke well for how those people understood their task. The Sunday morning that young couple was before the congregation to be voted upon was special. One of the older members of the church said to me afterwards that it was the happiest day he had ever experienced as a member of that congregation. It was happy for me, too. I looked forward to being home for a while. During the 17 months in Madera, I was only able to get home every two weeks for a day and a half. Anne and I looked forward to having some time together.

Anne had gone back into nursing. Marshall Hospital had offered a refresher course for nurses who had been inactive, and Anne decided to take part. I admire her willingness to do that. After being away from nursing for 19 years it had to be like starting all over. Trying to learn of all the new medications had to be almost overwhelming in itself. However, she never moaned about it in letters she wrote, or when I was home on my day off. I forget now how many weeks that retraining took, but by the time I had finished at Madera, she was working four days a week at Marshall.

My first project was to build a woodshed on the south side of the house. I knew very little about building things beyond which edge of the saw did the cutting. It took me quite a while, but I finally completed the job. A carpenter would quickly see that an amateur had done the work, but to this amateur it looked fine. Not only so, it kept two cords of wood dry during the winter months. By the time that job was completed I began to wonder why Bob Graham hadn't called about another interim ministry. Anne's salary kept us financially afloat, but I began to feel uncomfortable with me not contributing. As I look back, I now wonder why I didn't go to Sacramento and talk with Bob Graham. As weeks, then months went by with no word from the Mission Area office I began to wonder if in going into interim ministry I had committed vocational suicide.

Then one day, Bob's secretary, Helene called. She said that the Exeter church in San Joaquin Presbytery was in the process of seeking an interim pastor, and wondered if I would preach at one of the Sacramento churches on the following Sunday and meet with the committee afterwards. My immediate feeling was that I really didn't want to be that far from home. Exeter is south of Fresno, and closer to Los Angeles than it is to where we lived. However, also in mind was the thought, "how can I claim to be a follower of Jesus, if I am not open to a call?" So I thanked Helene, and told her I would be glad to preach in Sacramento. She said she would contact the chairman of the committee and get back to me. It was many hours later that she called. The gist of what she told me was that she had been working on the thing all day. There was no way the committee would come to Sacramento, so she had arranged for me to preach at a Presbyterian church in Fresno, and meet with the committee afterwards. What a downer that was! I didn't want to be an interim pastor in Exeter. I most certainly didn't want to go to Fresno to preach, and then meet with a committee. To do that meant I would have to go to Fresno on Saturday, find out where the church building was, and get a motel close at hand so that I would be sure to be on time for Sunday morning services. At the same time, I had the awareness that Helene had been working all day to arrange this. How could I say that I didn't care to do that, and ever expect to be asked again? Feeling trapped, I thanked Helen, and said I would be in Fresno the following Sunday. Fortunately, Anne had the weekend off, and was able to make the trip with me. It was a four-hour drive to Fresno. Looking at a map, I saw that it would be another hour's drive to get to Exeter. That confirmed my feeling of not wanting to be that far from home. From that distance I would again be unable to get home more often than every two weeks. I preached the next morning, thanked the pastor for allowing me to do that, and met with the committee made up of likeable people. Among other things that were discussed, it became clear that there had been unhappiness with their pastor, and they had fired him. After the 17 months at Madera, trying to help those people deal with the anger, and the hurt, and the guilt related to a situation in which the pastoral relationship is forcibly severed, I knew that I didn't want to be in that kind of situation again. You probably are seeing the handwriting on the wall. The Session in Exeter, acting upon their committee's recommendation, asked me to be their interim pastor.

What can I say about the two years as interim pastor in Exeter that would be of interest to anyone else? When I drove away from home it was with a lump in my throat. Arriving in Exeter after five hours of driving didn't do a thing toward easing that lump. Unlike the Sunesons in Madera, no one had reached out to welcome me. Apart from the members of the committee, with whom I had met for about two-hours, I was a stranger among strangers. The first night I spent in the local motel. As first order of business the next day I rented an apartment in Visalia, ten miles from Exeter. Nothing closer was available. Fortunately for me the very next month, an apartment one block from the church building became available. Laura Heaton, a member of the church, owned the apartment and arranged for me to rent it. By then, I was getting to know people, and they were getting to know me. Ruth Graves, a fine lady, saw to it that the apartment was furnished comfortably with items loaned by people of the congregation. You know how it is with a small town. Unless one is born there, the natives tend to think of a person as an outsider. Nevertheless, having that apartment in town, I felt more a part of things.

Exeter is in the heart of Southern California orange growing country, beautiful large unfenced orchards all along those country roads. There is a big Sunkist Plant in town. One of the members of the church, Curtis Dungan, owned several large orchards. Not long after we met, he was showing me around, and he said that I was welcome to fill a box from his trees to take with me when I went home every two weeks. Years earlier I had read *The Grapes of Wrath,* and of hungry people taking fruit from trees along the road when they got to California, and the ranchers not taking kindly to that. Mr. Dungan went on to say that if any of his employees questioned me picking oranges I just needed to tell them I had his permission. I said,

"They won't shoot first and then ask questions after will they?"

"Not if you ain't a Methodist," he replied. How nice it was to be able to laugh with him. Whoever coined the phrase, "laughter, the best medicine" knew what he was talking about.

Anne and I have concluded that we are survivors. Insofar as that is true of me I have my mother to thank. Under very trying circumstances, by example, she taught her children how to take what comes along and survive. Did the two years I spent as their pastor make any positive difference in the life of that Presbyterian congregation in Exeter? I am guessing that would depend upon whom you asked. As it would be for any couple with a good relationship, the two years was difficult for us. As mentioned, I was able to go home for a day off every two weeks. That meant a round trip of ten hours cooped up in an automobile. The five-hour drive home was easier than the five hours driving back. I'd crawl into that steel cocoon and vegetate. Every six months Anne was able to come back with me and spend the two-week period, thanks to her nurse manager. That helped considerably.

My brother Denis and I correspond regularly. Mom was staying with our sister Pat for the past few years since she was no longer able to stay alone. Denis suggested that it would make way more sense for me to visit while she was still alive, rather than go back for a funeral. It did make sense, so I began to plan to do that when I had completed the interim at Exeter. When I accepted the invitation to be interim pastor, my intention was to stay with the congregation until a new pastor had been called. The amount of time involved in the process was averaging a year throughout the denomination. As the end of my second year drew near, I decided it would be a good time to terminate the relationship. It seemed to me that the pastor seeking committee was taking unusually long in the search for a new pastor. Consequently, I informed the members of the Session that I was resigning when the two years was completed. So it was that my work with the First Presbyterian Church of Exeter ended. Frankly, I felt worn out, emotionally more than physically. Being away from home so much, the wearing trips in-between, along with the every day demands of ministry had all taken their toll. Ordinarily, annual periods of vacation time would work their restorative magic. There was nothing keeping me from taking vacations except my personal feeling about that. If one is only going to be on the scene for a year, it doesn't make sense to be gone for a month. That is too disruptive of a congregation's routine, already upset by the loss of their pastor. I had no way of knowing that my stay at Exeter would last for two years.

Anne came down to help me move. Not so much because there was a great deal of things to move, but just to be with me. Neither of our children lived at home anymore. Glenn had joined the Navy right after he graduated from high school. Karen had taken a job in a doctor's office, and was living in town. The long period between ending at Madera, and beginning at Exeter led me to think there would be plenty of time for me to be renewed. It made sense to us, for me to visit in Connecticut, and get that in back of us. So I made arrangements with Denis for a three-week visit. It had been nine years since last I saw any of them. At the time, Denis was upset with both sisters, which is something not at all unusual. You would have to know us to understand. The three weeks, by the way, was part of a promotion by the airline that gave me cheaper fare. It was necessary for me to stay the three weeks. Denis had suggested that I not visit either of our sisters, his way of socking it to them for whatever he was angry about. Of course, I reminded him that my reason for going back was to visit with each of them. Within a week of my arrival Denis was angry with me, too. But because of the airline he was stuck with me. We were stuck with each other. We visited with Joan one day. Then we spent an afternoon with Pat and family, my mom. Denis and I played cribbage, spent a day in our old hometown, but the air between us was icy. We are very much alike in many ways. I went there as a brother, he received me as a guest, and before the three weeks were up I felt like a stranger. Even though we settled all that years ago, and are back to exchanging weekly letters, I feel some tension as I write about it. If you were talking with Denis, and I came up in the conversation, Denis would give me high praise, and he would be meaning what he was saying. Nonetheless, I suspect that if I went to stay with him for a while, he would be angry with me within a week. It was a major relief to get back on that airplane and head for home.

I was anticipating some quality time at home, free from pressure. The day after I returned from Connecticut Bob Graham called. He said that Geneva Presbyterian Church in Modesto was in need of an interim pastor. With a grin in his voice, he mentioned the three weeks in which I had time to get rested, and asked if I would be willing to meet with the Ministerial Relations Committee of Stockton Presbytery and talk about the situation. The same kind of thought went through my mind, "How can I claim to be open to call if I am unwilling to talk to a committee?" Arrangements were made, and the two of us drove down to Stockton to meet with the committee. Only two of them were present. The main topic was Geneva Presbyterian Church, and how the congregation was in need of healing. There had been a great deal of tension, and the pastoral relationship severed. They had fired their pastor! After listening for a while, I said, "I've just completed a difficult two years in Exeter. I feel worn out, my battery plates are all buckled. Consequently, I would need to have a greater sense of call than I have right now, in order for me to agree to go to Geneva Church." One of the members of the committee said, "I hope you get that sense of call. They need you." I thanked them and went home thinking that was the end of the matter.

Two weeks later I received another call from Bob Graham wondering what had happened with the committee in Stockton. I told him what had taken place. He asked if I would be willing to talk with the committee from Geneva. The old question once again in my mind, "how could I be unwilling, and be honest with my commitments?" Arrangements were made, Anne and I drove down to Modesto to meet with the committee at Geneva Presbyterian. A distinguished looking man met us in the parking lot. He introduced himself, and then led us to the sanctuary. The people who designed that place of worship knew something about reverence. I was impressed. Something else had struck me favorably. It only took us an hour and forty-five minutes to get there from home. We were then taken to the church office, and introduced to the members of the committee. One of the women present was not a member of the committee. She just wanted to be there. That is a bit unusual, but since it clearly wasn't a problem for the committee members, it most certainly was no problem for me. In fact I thought it somewhat refreshing that someone in the congregation cared enough to invest her time when she didn't have to.

The chairman of the committee began by saying that I should be proud of the recommendations made to the committee on my behalf. He went on to say that apart from the recommendations they really didn't know anything else about me, and asked me to tell them about myself. That was dangerous on his part. Have you noticed that ministers as a group tend towards being very wordy? Not only so, opening the door for a person to talk about themselves can lead to large amounts of time being consumed. So I said, "I think I may be able to save all of us a lot of time. In order for me to be your interim pastor I would need $2,000 monthly. Also, I would need two days off weekly to spend at home." I was fairly sure that the interview would end there. But it didn't, there were questions and answers. After a while the chairman asked one of the men if he would take Anne and me to another room while the committee talked. In a relatively short time they sent for us. The chairman said that my conditions were acceptable, and that they would like to know my answer within 48 hours. I thanked them, asked if they knew of a restaurant they would recommend that was on our way out of town. They did, and we stopped there to eat dinner. While we were eating I said to Anne that I didn't know how something would feel more like a call. She agreed and when we arrived home I called the chairman of the committee and told him I didn't need 48 hours, I would be pleased to be their interim pastor. We agreed on a starting date, about a week from then as I recall. During that week he called to say that there was some confusion about salary with some of the committee members. They were thinking in terms of $1,700 a month. I replied that I would certainly not hold it against them if they wanted to back out of the invitation, but that I had tried to make clear the salary I needed was $2,000 a month. He said that would be no problem, and the invitation stood. He went on to say that Geneva had an assistant pastor, and that he was feeling somewhat left out in the process of an interim pastor being called. The chairman suggested that it could smooth potentially troubled waters if I would make a point of driving down just to meet with Jerry. So I did that.

I found Jerry Andrews, the assistant pastor, to be a personable young man. I have little idea of what he found me to be, but he was stuck with me, and made the most of it. We agreed to meet regularly to talk about what we were feeling in our shared work. I asked him how often he would like to preach at Sunday services. He said that he thought once monthly would be good. So we proceeded on that basis.

After I had been on the scene for several weeks, the distinguished looking man who had met Anne and me in the parking lot, stopped by my office. He said that there were people who felt that Jerry should be terminated. He wondered what I thought about that. I told him that I had a feeling that Jerry was going to be making a move in the not too distant future. If he was terminated by the Session there was required responsibility to pay his salary for six months, but if he was allowed to make a move he would leave with good feelings about himself, and in the meanwhile he would continue his work for the church. That made sense to my visitor, and that's how the matter rested. I never mentioned that to Jerry.

During our regular meetings Jerry mentioned that he was thinking seriously of trying to find a church in Washington. I don't recall now whether he, or his wife, or both of them had been raised in the western part of that State.

The months went by, Jerry received a call from a Presbyterian Church in Sequim, Washington. He preached his farewell sermon on Easter Sunday. There was a congregational get together after the service at which gifts were given to Jerry and his family. For unknown reasons the people of the church did not hold monthly potluck dinners, reasons unknown to me, that is.

According to the way I operated, it was not up to the interim pastor to begin new programs. Rather, it was up to me to do the things that would make it smoother for the new pastor when he or she arrived. That arrival took place a year after Jerry left. The congregation issued a call to a man and woman ministerial team. I led the congregation in worship for the last time, Easter Sunday, 1987. That was the last sermon I ever preached. Anne was in agreement with my feeling that it was time to retire. A feeling that had grown through working with three different congregations, each of which had fired their pastors.

My 62nd birthday was in September. Anne agreed to keep working until I was eligible for Medicare. That made it possible for me to retire. If something had come up regarding further ministry during the four and a half months prior to that date I would have responded, but nothing did. The necessary work was done with Sacramento Presbytery, the Board of Pensions, and Social Security to confirm my retirement. Many years have elapsed since those first pension checks arrived.

Those years have been a long sabbatical in which to catch up. Do you know what I mean? All those prior years, caught up in the stuff of life. Earliest years spent in the Depression Era, thirty-nine months as a sailor during WW II, living the agony of a marriage rooted in stupidity, making a commitment to follow Jesus, attending college, then seminary. I lived the differing roles of husband, parent, and pastor. As instance of what I mean by "catching up": very seldom, if ever, during all of those years did I think about my part in WW II. Being retired changed that. I thought of much from out of the past. There was the bombardment of Shimizu, for example.

When we carried out that mission I thought it was one of a kind; Seven Destroyers going 35 miles inside a Japanese harbor. The Squadron Commander said that it was the deepest penetration of Japanese waters during the war. In thinking about it now, I wondered why Admiral Halsey had placed seven ships, and 2,500 sailors at such risk just six days before the atom bomb was dropped. What we did that night had little to do with hastening the end of the war. Samuel Elliot Morrison in volume 14 of his extensive history of that war, mentions the raid in a brief paragraph, saying that it had little military value. I admired Admiral Halsey, and I am proud to have sailed under his command. It occurred to me that perhaps the Admiral hadn't been told of the atom bomb. Reading his biography, however, I discovered that he had been told several days before we made the raid. Then I learned that I was able to obtain copies of the Squadron Commander's report for that period, and Admiral Halsey's report, from the National Archives. I discovered, that rather than being a one of a kind mission, ours was one of ten similar actions. In his report, Admiral Halsey tells of his thinking. "A policy of sweeps by light forces was stressed in order to keep pressure on the enemy, to probe for weaknesses and reaction, to tighten the blockade, to adversely affect enemy morale, and to inflict damage." That made sense to me, and I now understood why we had been put at risk that night. That understanding was something of serendipity that came out of my search.

I have been in correspondence with a Japanese lady who was present in Shimizu when we bombarded. Kimiko Mochizuki was in her teens that night, as was I. Presently she is the leader of Shimizu International Friendship Association, and that is how I was able to contact her. She told me that 44 people were killed that night, and approximately 80 people injured, 35 of them seriously. Just numbers on a page now, but once individual persons who loved, and hoped, and were afraid, and all of a sudden one night injured or killed. There in microcosm is portrayed the insanity of war. People killing each other, or at least trying to, supposedly to solve some major problems. The only thing of it is, dead people can't solve anything. One of the hit songs from that period was *"There'll be Bluebirds Over the White Cliffs of Dover".* Part of the verse went, *"there'll be love and laughter, and peace ever after."* When the war ended I thought it would happen that way. That never again would mankind engage in that awful waste of people and resources. Years later I learned that the Ringgold had become the property of West Germany, people who had been the enemy when I was spending three years of my life on that ship. At the time I was driving a Japanese made automobile, the quality of which was impressive. I wondered to myself, who really won that war? My personal conclusion is that nobody won, not really, and a whole lot of people lost, and some more horribly than others. The sum of the years I have lived has resulted in a deep sense of longing:

For a world
In which children grow up unafraid
Where no one would think
Of doing harm to a child,
Neither physically,
Nor emotionally,
And most certainly not sexually.
Everyone has enough to eat,
Decent shelter,
And an honest way to earn
The things necessary for living.
The efforts of all
Spent upon creating,
Rather than destroying.
Building up,
Rather than tearing down.
Making things to enhance life,
Rather than to hurt, or maim or kill.
The air is clean,
The water, too.
War???
Just a memory
Of a primitive past!
And all people,
Able to live with dignity,
Because liberty, and justice, and peace,
Are real.

0-595-28206-7